I Have Called You by Name

The Stories of
16 Saints and Christian Heroes

by

Patricia Mitchell

the WORD among us

The Word Among Us
9639 Doctor Perry Road
Ijamsville, Maryland 21754
ISBN: 0-932085-37-7
www.wordamongus.org

Cover design by David Crosson

Made and printed in the United States of America

Library of Congress Cataloging-in-Publication Data

Mitchell, Patricia, 1953-
        I have called you by name: the stories of 16 saints and Christian
heroes/by Patricia Mitchell.
                p.   cm.
    Includes bibliographical references.
    ISBN 0-932085-37-7 (pbk.:alk.paper)
            1.   Christian saints—Biography. 2. Catholics—Biography. I. Title.

BX4655.2 .M58 2000
282'.092'2—dc21
[B]

Table of Contents

Introduction

"Fear not, for I have redeemed you; I have called you by name, you are mine." Isaiah 43:1

In a dramatic way, the lives of the saints make it clear that God has a plan for all of his people. He creates us, he redeems us, and he calls us by name—lovingly and intimately. As the saints responded to that call, their lives unfolded in very different ways. Some endured more suffering than others; some became well-known while others lived in obscurity. Clearly, God's plan is not the same for each person. Whatever happened to them, however, the saints show us what God can do when we answer his call wholeheartedly, without reservation or doubt.

Over the past two thousand years of Christianity, God has raised up countless saints. Most have remained anonymous. But in those whose stories have been kept alive and who have been honored by the church, we have a priceless treasure. As we take the time to become familiar with these saints, we discover real men and women who faced many of the same obstacles and difficulties we encounter in our own lives. We can learn from them—how they kept burning an intense love and zeal for God, how they persevered and stayed the course, how they summoned up the courage to face opposition, sickness and death. Ultimately, they teach us about our Father, who abounds in steadfast love and mercy and who always keeps his promises to us.

The saints and Christian heroes in this book stretch across the years—from Ignatius of Antioch, a first-century bishop who faced the lions in Rome, to Blessed Miguel Augustín Pro, a twentieth-century priest who faced an execution squad in Mexico City. With each biography is a timeline of the saint's life and a selection from his or her writings or, when one was unavailable, an excerpt written about the saint by someone else.

In each case, our goal is that our readers come to know the saints in their humanity. From a distance, we can keep saints as wooden as their statues. As we read about the events of their lives as well as what they wrote, they jump from the page. They become our friends and mentors, our brothers and sisters in Christ.

Many thanks to Leo Zanchettin, editor of *The Word Among Us Magazine*, who contributed the biography of Henri Lacordaire, and to Jeanne Kun, staff writer for *The Word Among Us*, who contributed the biography of Paul Couturier.

Let us raise our hearts to the Lord in gratitude for calling his saints by name. Let us pray that as we keep the memory of these great witnesses before us, we too will respond to Christ's call in our lives.

Patricia Mitchell
The Word Among Us

Late Have I Loved You

Saint Augustine of Hippo

354 - 430

I t was an adolescent prank—
pears stolen from a neighbor's tree. But as Augustine looked
back on the incident many years later, it seemed reprehen-
sible to him. He had no need of the pears; they were thrown
to the pigs. It was the thrill of committing theft with his
friends that he had sought. "My feasting was only on the
wickedness which I took pleasure in enjoying" (*Confessions*,
Book II, 12).

St. Augustine wrote the story of his conversion more than
sixteen hundred years ago, but this distance in time does not
dilute the immediacy of his struggle—or of his ultimate victory. A brilliant and passionate young man who vigorously
sought the truth, Augustine was lured by the temptations of
the flesh and the vanities of the world. After an intense battle of the will, he discovered the truth of Christ and the power
of the cross to overcome sin. The heart of his journey to God

was captured famously in the opening to his book, the *Confessions*: "You have made us for yourself, O Lord, and our heart is restless until it rests in you" (I,1).

Augustine lived under the rule of the Roman Empire. He was born in 354 in the African province of Numidia, now eastern Algeria. His mother, Monica, was a devout Christian; his father, Patricius, a landowner and a pagan. Although the family was not rich, they were able to send Augustine to good schools.

Outdoing His Friends in Sin

At the age of sixteen, Augustine was forced to wait a year in his hometown of Thagaste while his father scraped up enough money to send him to the university in Carthage. This year was spent in idleness and sin. "I went on my way headlong with such blindness that among my peer group I was ashamed not to be equally guilty of shameful behavior when I heard them boasting of their sexual exploits," Augustine wrote (II,7).

In Carthage, Augustine was at the top of his class in rhetorical studies, pleased with his success and "inflated with conceit" (III,6). He became captivated by the theater. However, when he was eighteen, he read Cicero's *Hortensius*, and it changed the direction of his life: "Suddenly every vain hope became empty to me, and I longed for the immortality of wisdom with an incredible ardor in my heart" (III,7). He picked up the Bible, but felt it inferior to Cicero, whose grand style far outstripped the awkward Latin biblical translation then in common use. Instead, Augustine became a Manichee.

The Manichees claimed to be authentic Christians, but

they denied the reality of the humanity of Christ, venerated the sun and moon as divine, and taught that their founder, Mani, was the Paraclete. They believed that evil in the world was a result of a great battle between the kingdoms of light and darkness. Since the Manichees considered evil to be a force outside of themselves, they did not have to take responsibility for their own transgressions. As Augustine later explained, "I still thought it is not we who sin, but some alien nature which sins in us" (V,18).

Augustine returned to his hometown at the age of nineteen. Monica was outraged when she discovered that her son was a Manichean and at first refused to let him into the house, but on the advice of a good bishop, she relented. Augustine set himself up as a teacher of rhetoric, settled down with his mistress, who had borne him a son, and became interested in astrology. He was shaken to the core, however, when a very close friend died. Overcome by despair, Augustine found that "everything on which I set my gaze was death" (IV,9). He could not stay in Thagaste any longer; everything reminded him of his friend. At the age of twenty-two, he took his mistress and young son to Carthage where he could teach.

As the years progressed, Augustine began to question some of the more outlandish teachings of the Manichees as well as the unscientific basis of astrology. When he was twenty-nine, he decided to go to Rome to teach, where the students were reported to be less rowdy than in Carthage. Monica was so upset over his departure that Augustine had to slip away while she slept. She continued to beg the Lord to bring her son to him and took comfort from a dream that he would someday become a Christian.

The Light Begins to Dawn

The students were quieter in Rome, but they also went to other tutors when it was time to pay their bills. Consequently, Augustine applied to become a teacher of rhetoric for the city of Milan and was accepted. There he met the devout and highly regarded bishop, Ambrose. At first Augustine was attracted to Ambrose's rhetorical style, but slowly the bishop's message began to penetrate his heart. Augustine realized that he had misjudged many of the church's doctrines. He also found he could accept difficult passages in the Old Testament when Ambrose explained them. Augustine decided to become a catechumen in the Catholic Church, but he was not entirely convinced. He still waited for "some clear light" to come to him (V,25).

Monica soon joined her son in Milan, where she found him severely depressed. As Augustine wrote, "I had lost all hope of discovering the truth" (VI,1). Monica redoubled her petitions, and arranged for a suitable marriage for Augustine, convinced that once married, he would be baptized. A young girl from a good family was found, but Augustine had to wait two years until she reached the minimum age for marriage under Roman law. He sent his mistress back to Carthage because she was a hindrance to the impending marriage, which was an exquisitely painful separation for both of them: "My heart which was deeply attached was cut and wounded, and left a trail of blood" (VII,25). In the meantime, he took another mistress because, as he said, "I was a slave to lust" (VII,25).

Augustine continued his search for truth. He began to read the books of the Platonists, which helped him to realize that his original Manichean conceptions of God were flawed. The Platonic writings gave Augustine a glimpse of the true God and prepared his heart for the epistles of St. Paul. The problems he had earlier experienced with scripture "simply vanished" (VII,27).

A Battle of the Will

There still remained one last act for Augustine. He had to give up his old life, the way of sin and corruption, and embrace the life of grace. One day Augustine and his close friend Alypius were visited by an African official named Ponticianus, who told them about the life of St. Antony, the Egyptian who had lived as a monk. Friends of Ponticianus had been so inspired by the story of Antony that they immediately joined a monastery. As he listened, Augustine was filled with the shame and horror of his own sinfulness. "What is wrong with us?" he asked Alypius. "Uneducated people are rising up and capturing heaven, and we with all our dreary teachings—see where we roll in the mud of flesh and blood" (VIII,19).

Augustine retreated to the garden of the house where he was staying, tortured in heart and soul. The one necessary condition, he knew, was "the will to go" the narrow road (VIII,19), yet his will remained weak, unable to command him to take the final step to God. "I was hesitating whether to die to death and to live in life. Ingrained evil had more hold over me than unaccustomed good" (VIII,25). His "old loves" (VIII,26) held him back, whispering to him, reminding him of the things he would never experience again.

Augustine was distraught. He pulled on his hair, struck his forehead, and wept. Then, as he described it, "Lady

Continence" appeared to him in a vision—dignified, chaste, serene, and cheerful, "enticing me in an honorable manner to come and not hesitate" (VIII,27). Augustine saw throngs of men and women who had remained chaste, and the lady reminded him that God had given them this grace.

Suddenly, he heard a voice, like that of a young child, chanting, "pick up and read, pick up and read" (VIII,29). He interpreted this as a command from God, and picked up the Bible, opening immediately to this passage: "Not in riots and drunken parties, not in eroticism and indecencies, not in strife and rivalry, but put on the Lord Jesus Christ and make no provision for the flesh in its lusts" (Romans 13:13-14). Peace flooded Augustine's heart. "It was as if a light of relief from all anxiety flooded into my heart. All the shadows of doubt were dispelled" (VIII.29). He and Alypius made resolutions to live in the light of Christ, and immediately went to tell Monica, who was overjoyed.

At the end of the school term, Augustine left his teaching position and spent his vacation at the country estate of a friend. He returned to Milan and in April 387, at the age of thirty-two, was baptized and received into the church. Augustine, his son Adeodatus, his mother, and his friends agreed to return to Africa. Along the way in Ostia, near Rome, Monica died.

Augustine reached Africa in 388. In 391, in the cathedral at Hippo, the congregation brought him before Bishop Valerius to be ordained. He founded a monastery at Hippo, entered into public debates with the Manichees, and wrote tirelessly in defense of the Catholic faith. In 395 he became Bishop of Hippo. He was a prolific writer, and wrote his two most famous books while bishop—the *Confessions* and *The City of God*. His theological works remain the basis for many important Christian beliefs and doctrines. He died peacefully on August 28, 430, at the age of seventy-six.

"Late have I loved you, beauty so old and so new: late have I loved you," Augustine wrote in his *Confessions* (X,38). Augustine's journey to God took longer than he may have wished, but the Lord wasted no time in transforming Augustine's natural passion, energy and brilliance to serve him and his church. Monica's unceasing prayers had been answered beyond her wildest expectations.

Late Have I Loved You

This selection is taken from Book IX of
St. Augustine's *Confessions*, in which
he describes his feelings about the death
of his mother Monica.
The book is addressed to God.

On the ninth day of her illness, when she was aged fifty-six, and I was thirty-three, this religious and devout soul was released from the body.

I closed her eyes and an overwhelming grief welled into my heart and was about to flow forth in floods of tears. But at the same time under a powerful act of mental control my eyes held back the flood and dried it up. The inward struggle put me into great agony. Then when she breathed her last, the boy Adeodatus cried out in sorrow and was pressed by all of us to be silent. In this way too something of the child in me, which had slipped towards weeping, was checked and silenced by the youthful voice, the voice of my heart. We did not think it right to celebrate the funeral with tearful dirges and lamentations, since in most cases it is customary to use such mourning to imply sorrow for the miserable state of those who die, or even their complete extinction. But my mother's dying meant neither that her state was miserable nor that she was suffering extinction. We were confident of this because of the evidence of her virtuous life, her "faith unfeigned" (1 Timothy 1:15), and reasons of which we felt certain.

Why then did I suffer sharp pains of inward grief? It must have been the fresh wound caused by the break in the habit formed by our living together, a very affectionate and precious bond suddenly torn apart. I was glad indeed to have her testimony when in that last sickness she lovingly responded to my attentions by calling me a devoted son. With much feeling in her love, she recalled that she had never heard me speak a harsh or bitter word to her. And yet, my God our maker, what comparison can there be between the respect with which I deferred to her and the service she rendered to me? Now that I had lost the immense support she gave, my soul was wounded, and my life as it were torn to pieces, since my life and hers had become a single thing. . . .

From then on, little by little, I was brought back to my old feelings about your handmaid, recalling her devout attitude to you and her holy gentle and considerate treatment of us, of which I had suddenly been deprived. I was glad to weep before you about her and for her, about myself and for myself. Now I let flow the tears which I had held back so that they ran as freely as they wished. My heart rested upon them, and it reclined upon them because it was your ears that were there, not those of some human critic who would put a proud interpretation on my weeping. And now, Lord, I make my confession to you in writing. Let anyone who wishes read and interpret as he pleases. If he finds fault that I wept for my mother for a fraction of an hour, the mother who had died before my eyes who had wept for me that I might live before your eyes, let him not mock me but rather, if a person of much charity, let him weep himself before you for my sins; for you are the Father of all the brothers of your Christ. ⪻⊙⪼

The Life of Augustine of Hippo

354 - Born on November 13 in Thagaste, in the Roman province of Numidia

370 - Goes to Carthage to study at the university

372 - Reads Cicero's *Hortensius* and it changes the direction of his life; birth of a son, Adeodatus, with his Carthage mistress

373 - Returns to Thagaste to teach rhetoric; becomes a Manichee

376 - Saddened by the loss of a close friend, leaves Thagaste to teach in Carthage, taking his mistress and son with him

383 - Goes to Rome to teach

384 - Becomes professor in Milan; reads Platonic books; Monica joins him

386 - Experiences conversion in July

387 - Baptized and received into the church in April; Monica dies on way back to Africa

389 - Adeodatus dies at age seventeen

391 - Ordained a priest in the cathedral at Hippo

395 - Named Bishop of Hippo

397-400 - Writes *Confessions*

430 - Dies on August 28 in Hippo at age seventy-six

I Have Called You by Name

Let Nothing Disturb You

Saint Teresa of Avila

1515 - 1582

In Your Hand
I place my heart,
Body, life and soul,
Deep feelings and affections mine.
Spouse—Redeemer sweet,
Myself offered now to You.

Very early one November morning in 1535, as the light cast soft shadows on the austere Castilian landscape, twenty-year-old Teresa de Ahumada y Cepeda stole away from her home in Avila. Her destination— the Carmelite Convent of the Incarnation in the same city. Her heart ached that morning at the thought of leaving her widowed father behind. "It seemed that every bone in my body was being sundered," she later wrote.

The decision had not been easy. Teresa's father, Don Alonso, was a devout and wealthy nobleman who loved his daughter deeply and didn't want to see her leave home. Even worse, Teresa was ambivalent about becoming a nun. She had spent several years in a convent as a boarder and enjoyed the experience. She knew that this environment was better for her than the vanities and frivolities she had indulged in with her cousins. Still, she had never felt a strong desire to enter a convent. In the end, she confessed, "I was moved more by servile fear than by love."

Over many years, God was to transform that fear into the heights of mystical love. Teresa of Avila's works on prayer are considered to be some of the greatest pieces of spiritual literature ever composed. Teresa was also a woman of action who pioneered a reform of the Carmelite religious order at great personal cost.

As soon as Teresa arrived at the Incarnation convent, she felt a great peacefulness about her decision. The beautiful woman with the curly chestnut hair, dancing dark eyes, and vivacious personality could have had her choice of suitors, yet she was content with her new life. However, after only a few years at the convent, Teresa became very ill, and her father took her to her sister's house in search of a cure.

On the way, Teresa stopped to visit her uncle. He gave her a book on prayer that went beyond the vocal recitations that Teresa was used to in the convent. She devoured it, realizing that through prayer she could enjoy a deep friendship and intimacy with God she had never thought possible.

Happy the enamored heart,
Thought centered on God alone,
Renouncing every creature for Him,
Finding in Him glory and contentment.
Living forgetful of self,
In God is all its intention.

Teresa's prayer life should have been progressing, but in

1542, she halted any attempts to practice mental prayer. She was convinced that her sins were too great, and the casual environment of the convent was too distracting. Visitors were regularly received in the convent parlor, and Teresa, a lively conversationalist, was always in demand. Many of the nuns wore jewelry, accepted gifts, and were permitted to leave the convent for long periods of time. Teresa felt that she had allowed her soul "to become so spoiled by many vanities." In 1544, while Teresa was nursing her dying father, her confessor convinced her to return to prayer.

For the next eleven years, Teresa lived the ordinary life of a nun but still felt like a failure: "On the one hand, God was calling me. On the other, I was following the world. All the things of God made me happy; those of the world held me bound." Prayer was dry, Teresa said later, because "I was not able to shut myself within myself . . . instead, I shut within myself a thousand vanities."

One day in 1555, after she had been a nun for twenty years, Teresa entered the oratory and saw a borrowed statute of the wounded Christ. "I felt so keenly aware of how poorly I thanked him for those wounds that, it seems to me, my heart broke." Surrendering herself to God, she begged him for help. From then on, she was able to make discernible progress in prayer—even to the point of experiencing great "delights and favors" from God. Teresa said she had received a new life, no longer her own, but one in which God lived in her.

Over the next several years, God granted Teresa so many experiences of his presence in prayer that she feared she was being misled by the devil. Visions and raptures occurred frequently—even in front of the other nuns, which humiliated her. In one vision, an angel pierced Teresa's heart with a spear, and as he withdrew it, she was left "completely afire with a great love for God." Throughout her life, she could not understand why God had granted her such favors. She always felt radically unworthy of them.

Even as Teresa experienced union with the Lord, she never lost touch with her own humanity. Affectionate and lively, she often became very attached to others. She wrote to one prioress, "I assure you that if you love me dearly, I love you in return and like to hear you tell me so." Neither was she beyond castigating her friends when they took too long to respond to her letters. Even with the Lord she was completely honest. Once, when God told her to bring a message to someone, she replied, "Why do you give me this trouble? Can't you speak directly to him?"

> Untiring in loving,
> Our God is calling;
> Trusting Him, let us follow,
> *Nuns of Carmel*

One day in September 1560, Teresa and several other nuns were talking of the problems of living in such a large and undisciplined convent. Teresa's cousin, who was visiting, casually suggested that they start their own convent. The idea had already been stirring in Teresa's mind, and as she prayed about it, God told her it was the work he wanted her to do. Even her confessor agreed to the idea. The nuns at the Incarnation, however, felt threatened, and the people in Avila were none too eager to support another convent with alms.

Negotiating in secret through her sister Juana and using funds given her by a friend, Teresa purchased a house in the summer of 1561. Authorization was received in February 1562, and on August 24 of that year, the first Mass in St. Joseph's Convent was celebrated. The shock of a new convent stirred up residents, and the police tried unsuccessfully to gain entrance to the house. Several months later, Teresa was permitted to leave the Incarnation and join her four nuns in the first reformed house of the Carmelite order. For the next four years, God allowed Teresa to enjoy the serenity of St. Joseph's.

In 1567, the Carmelite General from Rome visited Teresa's convent and came away utterly impressed. The recent Council of Trent had encouraged the reform of religious orders, and here was one nun who was accomplishing it. He ordered Teresa to start more convents. She had nothing—the money, the houses, the people would all have to be found—but Teresa would rely on her natural astuteness and business sense to engineer the founding of sixteen more houses in her lifetime.

The second convent, in nearby Medina del Campo, produced the same opposition as the one in Avila. Teresa's solution was the same: The nuns took possession of the house in secret, after midnight. Once Mass had been celebrated early the next morning and the Blessed Sacrament installed, it was much more difficult to evict them.

> Let nothing disturb you
> Let nothing frighten you
> All things pass away:

God never changes.
Patience obtains all things.
He who has God
Finds he lacks nothing;
God alone suffices.

Each foundation presented its own set of challenges. As houses were founded in cities further away, Teresa and her nuns endured arduous rides in covered wagons, in blasting heat and cold winds, over dangerous mountain passes and flooded streams, often without water or food. Teresa was ill much of her life and often traveled with a fever. Worse, the inns where the nuns lodged at night were filthy and crowded.

Eventually, Teresa founded a branch of the reformed Carmelite order for men. One of her first friars was St. John of the Cross. Both the men's and women's reform movement inevitably ran into persecution from the Carmelites who remained under the more permissive rule. From 1576 to 1580, Teresa was forbidden to open new convents and was ordered to remain in Toledo. Finally, in June 1580, the reformed branch was recognized as a separate province, and Teresa was free to travel again.

During this time of persecution, Teresa wrote her spiritual masterpiece, *Interior Castle*. Writing under obedience to her confessor, she structured the book on a vision of "a most beautiful crystal globe, made in the shape of a castle, and containing seven mansions, in the seventh and innermost of which was the King of Glory." Teresa had experienced each of these stages—starting in the first mansion with the knowledge of her own sinfulness coupled with humility and gratitude at the great mercy of God. Along the way, as Teresa discovered, God's grace replaced her efforts to pray, and she became increasingly overwhelmed by divine love.

Teresa died on October 4, 1582, at the age of sixty-seven, exhausted by her work for the King who had come to live in her soul. In 1622 she was canonized, and in 1969, she was named a Doctor of the Church. Teresa of Avila, this most human of saints, had succeeded in communicating God's ardent desire for intimacy with the sons and daughters he created in love.

Let Nothing Disturb You

In her autobiography, *The Book of Her Life*, written under obedience to her superiors, St. Teresa of Avila used the analogy of watering a garden to explain four stages of prayer.

Beginners must realize that in order to give delight to the Lord they are starting to cultivate a garden on very barren soil, full of abominable weeds. His Majesty pulls up the weeds and plants good seed. Now let us keep in mind that all of this is already done by the time a soul is determined to practice prayer and has begun to make use of it. And with the help of God we must strive like good gardeners to get these plants to grow and take pains to water them so that they don't wither but come to bud and flower and give forth a most pleasant fragrance to provide refreshment for this Lord of ours. Then He will often come to take delight in this garden and find His joy among these virtues.

But let us see now how it must be watered so that we may understand what we have to do, the labor this will cost us, whether the labor is greater than the gain, and for how long it must last. It seems to me the garden can be watered in four ways. You may draw water from a well (which is for us a lot of work). Or you may get it by means of a water wheel and aqueducts in such a way that it is obtained by turning the crank of the water wheel. (I have drawn it this way sometimes—the method involves less work than the other, and you get more water.) Or it may flow from a river or a stream. (The garden is watered much better by this means because the ground is more fully soaked, and there is no need to water so frequently—and much less work for the gardener.) Or the water may be provided by a great deal of rain. (For the Lord waters the garden without any work on our part—and this way is incomparably better than all the others mentioned.)

Now, then, these four ways of drawing water in order to maintain this garden—because without water it will die—are what are important to me and have seemed applicable in explaining the four degrees of prayer in which the Lord in His goodness has sometimes placed my soul. . . .

Beginners in prayer, we can say, are those who draw water from the well. This involves a lot of work on their own part, as I have said. They must tire themselves in trying to recollect their senses. Since they are accustomed to being distracted, this recollection requires much effort. They need to get accustomed to caring nothing at all about seeing or hearing, to practicing the hours of prayer, and thus to solitude and withdrawal—and to thinking on their past life. Although these beginners and the others as well must often reflect upon their past, the extent to which they must do so varies, as I shall say afterward. In the beginning such reflection is even painful, for they do not fully understand whether or not they are repentant of their sins. If they are, they are then determined to serve God earnestly. They must strive to consider the life of Christ—and the intellect grows weary in doing this.

These are the things we can do of ourselves, with the understanding that we do so by the help of God, for without this help as is already known we cannot have so much as a good thought. These things make up the beginning of fetching water from the well, and please God that it may be found. At least we are doing our part, for we are already drawing it out and doing what we can to water these flowers. God is so good that when for reasons His Majesty knows—perhaps for our greater benefit—the well is dry and we, like good gardeners, do what lies in our power, He sustains the garden without water and makes the virtues grow.

The Life of Teresa of Avila

1515 - Born in Avila on March 28 to a wealthy noble family

1528 - Teresa's mother dies

1531-32 - Becomes boarder at convent school of Our Lady of Grace

1535 - Enters Carmelite Convent of the Incarnation in Avila

1538 - Falls seriously ill; meets uncle and begins serious prayer life

1539 - Nearly dies, but recovers enough to return to Incarnation

1542 - Gives up mental prayer

1544 - Father dies; Teresa returns to prayer

1555 - Second conversion

1560 - Receives grace of the wounding of the heart; begins discussions of new foundation

1561 - Purchases house for St. Joseph's Convent in Avila in secret

1562 - First Mass at St. Joseph's Convent celebrated on August 24

1567 - Teresa authorized to start other reformed monasteries; foundation at Medina del Campo established on August 15; meets St. John of the Cross

1568-75 - Additional foundations established

1576 - Persecution of reformed order begins

1577 - Writes *Interior Castle*

1580 - Reformed Carmelites recognized as separate province

1582 - Dies on October 4 at monastery in Alba de Tormes

1622 - Canonized by Pope Gregory XV on March 12

1970 - First woman saint to be declared Doctor of the Church

I Have Called You by Name

The Undercover Priest

Blessed Miguel Augustín Pro

1891 - 1927

I n February 1927, with one stroke of the pen, Mexican President General Plutarco Elias Calles turned every priest in his country into an outlaw. He ordered them to leave their posts, wherever they were, and to report immediately to Mexico City. When they refused to obey, they faced arrest, imprisonment, and even death. Most went into hiding.

A young Jesuit priest, Father Miguel Augustín Pro, was already used to operating incognito. For two years, Calles had been enforcing harsh measures against the Catholic Church. The revolutionaries in power had overthrown an oppressive government and an unjust economic system more than a decade earlier. They considered the church a corrupt institution that had historically sided with the rich, not the poor. Now they wanted a national church controlled by the state.

The new laws forced priests to avoid the authorities by conducting Mass and hearing confessions secretly in private homes. Lay Catholics were also at risk of being thrown into prison if they were found to be harboring a priest.

Enthusiastically, Pro embraced the challenge to serve his people undercover. Always gifted at imitating others, he became a master of disguise. One day he would be a student, bouncing through the streets on his brother's old bicycle with a cigarette dangling from his mouth and a cap on his head. Another day he would be a car mechanic in overalls or a well-dressed dandy. In the end, however, Miguel Augustín Pro was executed for who he truly was— a servant of Christ and a minister to his people.

The Beginnings of a Vocation

Miguel Pro was born on January 13, 1891 in Zacatecas, a mining town in central Mexico where his father was an engineer. The conditions that would lead to the Mexican Revolution were already evident in the silver and gold mines in his hometown, where workers were poorly paid and badly treated. As a young boy, Miguel often accompanied his mother on missions of mercy, bringing the miners food, clothing, and medicine.

Miguel was a fun-loving child who played practical jokes on his family and wrote witty sonnets to his friends. When his two sisters announced that they were leaving home to enter the convent, he was heartbroken. Soon afterwards, however, he sensed that he too was being called to the religious life. He always felt that his vocation was a great gift from the Lord, one which he could never be worthy of on his own merits.

In 1911, at the age of twenty, Miguel entered the Jesuit order. In that same year, the longtime Mexican dictator, General Porfirio Diaz, was overthrown by a new revolutionary government led by Francisco Madero. From that point on, Pro's plans for the future were altered radically.

The pace of Madero's agrarian and social reforms failed to satisfy other revolutionaries in Mexico, who reignited the social unrest. Before long, revolutionary bandits banged on the door of the hacienda where Miguel and his fellow seminarians were living. On August 15, 1914, cassocks were replaced with clothing donated by farmers, and the seminarians went into hiding. Miguel sailed to Spain to resume his studies in a Jesuit house in Granada.

The civil unrest back home made correspondence difficult. Miguel often worried about his family, but he masked his heartache in playful jokes and fun. He polished his mimicry skills by imitating the odd mannerisms of one of his teachers; this earned him three days without recreation. He often volunteered to push the large cart of food into the dining room, where he pretended it was a car that he was driving. These pantomimes were closely watched by the other seminarians, who tried to keep from laughing aloud and drawing the attention of the rector.

Working for Justice

In 1920, Miguel was sent to Nicaragua to work at a boys' boarding school. Two years later, he traveled to Belgium to continue his studies. Pro's ability to connect

with working men and women made him extremely popular, and he became interested in the French Christian
social action movement, which he saw as a model for justice in Mexico. He was ordained in 1925 in Belgium, overjoyed even though no one in his family could attend the
ceremony. "At least we are priests," he told his friends, "and
that is enough."

Soon after, Miguel was sidelined by severe stomach pains
from bleeding ulcers. After three unsuccessful surgeries, he
was ordered back to Mexico with little hope for recovery. He
arrived in Mexico City in early July 1926 with a passport
marked "religious." Miraculously, no one in Customs took
notice, and he was allowed to enter the country.

The timing of his arrival could not have been better. On
July 31, 1926, the bishops of Mexico protested the government's oppression of the church by suspending all public worship requiring the participation of priests. People flocked to
churches for what they feared might be their last chance to
receive the sacraments, and Father Pro spent his first days
back in his homeland hearing confessions, celebrating
Mass, and performing baptisms and marriages.

"My poor carcass which has just left behind the soft pil-
lows of the hospital has not yet gotten used to the hard seat
of the confessional," he joked. Despite the workload,
however, his stomach troubles began to disappear. "My
health is like bronze," he later wrote to a friend.

Sacraments in Secret

Wearing his disguises, Father Pro began entering
homes using secret passwords and passing out Communion

to hundreds of people as they came in and out, trying not to draw the attention of the police. Many crowded together to hear his retreats and homilies. Pro was often in danger. Stepping outside of the house, he would light a cigarette and glance around to see who was waiting for him, before continuing.

Once, when he thought two men were following him, he hailed a taxicab and then asked the accommodating driver to slow down while he bailed out. As he stood leaning against a lamp post, the men, following in another cab, passed him right by. At another time, when he knew his pursuers were gaining on him, he whispered to a passing woman, "Help me, I'm a priest." They linked arms and were bypassed. He sometimes said his weapon was his crucifix and with it next to him, "I have no fear of anyone."

Periodically, Pro's superior would order him into hiding to avoid arrest. While using the time for theological study, Father Pro found it difficult to stay trapped in one place, especially when he knew how much he was needed. "Those who retain me here do not realize the fire that burns within me," he said.

A Desire for Martyrdom

Miguel's two younger brothers, Humberto and Roberto, were supporters of the *Cristeros*, a group that actively opposed the government's policies against the church. In December 1926, after the group released six hundred balloons filled with religious leaflets all over the city, the Pro home was raided. Miguel, the only one there, was arrested and sent to jail, but was released the next day.

The incident did nothing to inhibit him. Although he did not purposefully put himself in danger, Miguel longed for martyrdom. "The number of martyrs grows every day. Oh, if only I should draw a winning number," he wrote. If he did, he added, "get your prayers ready for heaven."

On November 13, 1927, a car formerly owned by Miguel's brothers was used in an assassination attempt on the newly elected president, General Alvaro Obregón. Five days later, Miguel and his two brothers—who had nothing to do with the incident—were arrested and thrown into prison. No trial took place.

On the morning of November 23, they were led outside the prison. Wanting to show the world the "cowardice" of a priest facing death, the government invited photographers and reporters to observe the event. Their plan would backfire spectacularly. Dressed in an old brown suit and tan sweater, Miguel Pro went to the wall and faced the firing squad. For a moment, he knelt down, prayed, and kissed his crucifix. Then, refusing a blindfold, he stood up with the crucifix in one hand and a rosary in the other, arms outstretched like the cross. Forgiving his enemies, he cried, "Viva Cristo Rey!"—"Long live Christ the King!" Five bullets entered his chest, and a final bullet to his head ended his life.

In defiance of the government, at least ten thousand people—crying "Viva Cristo Rey!"—lined the streets for Pro's funeral procession. Reports of miracles began to circulate even before Pro was buried.

The story of Miguel Pro's life destroys any typical notions of holiness: He was young, active, daring, and fun-loving. By laying down his life for his people, he brought courage and strength to thousands of Mexicans during a time of intense religious persecution. A witness of Jesus' sacrificial love, Miguel Augustín Pro was beatified on September 25, 1988.

The Undercover Priest

Bl. Miguel Pro wrote this poem on
the Feast of Christ the King,
begging the Lord to end the suffering
of the Mexican people.

Return in Haste, O Lord

O Lord, your empty tabernacles mourn
While we alone upon our Calvary,
As orphans, ask you, Jesus, to return
And dwell again within your sanctuary.

Since you have left your earthly door ajar,
Our lovely temples bare and dismal stand;
No chant of choir, no bells resound afar;
Dread silence hovers over our native land.

Our naves, once quivering with the mystic flight
Of prayer that fluttered as a heavenly breath,
Are now as silent as the somber night;
All seems oblivion, sadness, sleep and death.

O Lord, why has your presence from us fled?
Do you not remember how in days agone
Those countless hearts which in their trials bled
Found comfort in the light that from you shone?

Souls trembling with the thought of morrow's grief,
Souls crushed beneath the present cross of pain,
Souls tortured by the past—all found relief
Before the golden door. Oh! come again.

Afflicted, aged, orphan, pilgrim spent
With teasing struggles on life's darksome way;
The sick and those by cruel hunger bent,
And sinners burdened—all came here to pray.

To you beneath the sacramental veil
They fondly turned, and ever found relief;
For not a soul, however distressed, could fail
To draw from you sweet solace in its grief.

No grief could stay, no comfort be deferred,
No trial crush, when you were biding there;
In mystic sweetness still your voice was heard,
Whose accents shattered sin and banished care.

But now no longer do you dwell a King
Upon our altars, once as bright as day,
And we no more around you sweetly sing
Our anthems. Ah, how long will you from us stay?

The very breath of Hell floats in the air;
The cup of crime is filled by tyrant's hand;
And through the hideous gloom no dawning fair
Of hope is seen to glimmer over the land.

The barque of Peter on the stormy sea,
With Christ, our Leader, wrapt in peaceful sleep,
Seems well-nigh wrecked by man's iniquity,
That rages like a tempest over the deep.

Ah! Why do you abandon us, dear Lord?
A hymn repentant from our hearts we sing.
You cannot fail to keep your loving word;
   In Mexico the faithful hail you King.

Those who offended you but yesterday
Now tear-dimmed eyes turn trustfully to you;
With bleeding feet they went a pilgrim's way
From far and near to plead your clemency.

By the bitter tears of those who mourn their dead,
   By our martyrs' blood for you shed joyfully,
By crimson stream with which your heart has bled,
   Return in haste to your dear sanctuary.

The Life of Miguel Augustín Pro

1891 - Born on January 13 in Zacatecas, Mexico

1911 - Enters Jesuit order; Mexican dictator General Porfirio Diaz overthrown

1914 - Goes into hiding to avoid revolutionaries; sails to Granada, Spain, to resume studies

1920 - Works at boys' boarding school in Nicaragua

1925 - Ordained on August 31 in Belgium; suffers severe stomach ulcers

1926 - Arrives in Mexico City in July; arrested and jailed in December but released the next day

1927 - Murdered by government officials on November 23

1988 - Beatified by Pope John Paul II on November 25

The "Little Way" to God

Saint Thérèse of Lisieux

1873 - 1897

At the age of fifteen, Thérèse Martin entered a Carmelite monastery in Lisieux, France. Only nine years later, she died of tuberculosis in the same monastery. As uneventful as this may sound, within those walls, Sister Thérèse of the Child Jesus and the Holy Face received wisdom and grace beyond her years and left a powerful imprint upon the church that is still felt today. In her autobiography, *Story of a Soul*, Thérèse described her journey of faith as "the way of spiritual childhood, the way of trust and absolute surrender"—a way to God that anyone, at any time, could follow.

The Seeds of a Calling

Thérèse grew up in a prayerful and loving home. Born on January 2, 1873, she was the youngest of five daughters of Zelie and Louis Martin. "God was pleased all through my life to surround me with *love*, and the first memories I have are stamped with smiles and the most tender caresses,"

Thérèse wrote. A beautiful, intelligent, and strong-willed child, Thérèse was described by her mother as a "little imp" who "gets into frightful tantrums when things don't go just right."

Her idyllic childhood was shattered at the age of four, when her mother died of breast cancer. "My happy disposition completely changed after Mama's death," Thérèse wrote. "I, once so full of life, became timid and retiring, sensitive to an excessive degree." Needing to fill the void, Thérèse adopted her older sister Pauline as her new mother and remained very close to her father, whom she called her "king."

Spiritual conversation and devotions pervaded the Martin household, and Thérèse's love for God became an integral part of her being. Always attracted to the beauty in nature, she said that when she saw the ocean for the first time, "everything spoke to my soul of God's grandeur and power." Thus, the seeds for her own vocation were already planted by the time she heard that Pauline wanted to become a nun.

Healing for a Sensitive Soul

Still, when at nine, she learned that Pauline would be entering the Carmelite community in a matter of months, Thérèse was plunged into grief. She had always assumed that Pauline would wait for her to grow up. "It was as if a sword were buried in my heart," she wrote. "I was about to lose my second Mother."

Although she shined academically, Thérèse struggled in school because of her shy and reflective nature. She found

it very hard to relate to children her own age. It was not long
before the daily headaches and insomnia resulting from her
tension culminated in a complete breakdown. Thérèse's
family kept a bedside vigil while she suffered from hallu-
cinations and bodily tremors. Two months later, she saw a
"ravishing smile" on her statue of the Virgin Mary and
immediately began to recover.

In the midst of her sufferings, Thérèse felt more and
more drawn to Jesus, "my only friend." She saw her life as
a ship that would bring her to her true home, where she
would be reunited with her mother in heaven and with her
four brothers and sisters who had died in infancy.

When Thérèse was thirteen, her eldest sister Marie,
with whom she had grown very close, also left for Carmel.
Even at this age, Thérèse said, "I was really unbearable
because of my extreme touchiness." Much though she
longed to enter Carmel herself, she knew it would be
impossible until she stopped being so hypersensitive. She
also knew that she did not have the inner resources to
change. God had to work a miracle in her.

A Christmas Miracle

After returning from Christmas Midnight Mass that
year, Thérèse overheard her father—who was exhausted—
complain about having to stay up longer to watch his little girl open her gifts. Usually such a comment would have
made Thérèse dissolve into tears. But rather than give in
to her feelings, Thérèse found the strength to open her gifts
joyfully, as if she had never heard the remark. She realized
that God had accomplished "in one instant" what she had

tried to do for the last ten years on her own: "I felt *charity* enter into my soul, and the need to forget myself."

Even though she had only just turned fourteen, Thérèse now knew that God had prepared her for life in a cloistered community. She chose the feast of Pentecost in 1887 to tell her father. Louis Martin "cried out that God was giving him a great honor in asking his children from him," Thérèse wrote. Eventually, all five of his daughters would become nuns—four of them at the Carmelite monastery in Lisieux.

The road to Carmel was filled with obstacles. Thérèse's uncle urged her to wait until she was older, but several weeks later he unexpectedly changed his mind and told her that she was "a little flower God wanted to gather." Thérèse had always privately called herself God's little flower, so she knew her uncle's change of heart was a miracle. However, when the superior at Carmel refused to accept her because of her young age, Thérèse was devastated. She would have to go to the bishop for permission.

ʻOn a rainy day in late October, Thérèse and her father visited Bishop Flavien Hugonin. While waiting for him, the bishop's vicar general saw tears in her eyes and warned her not to "show her diamonds" to the bishop. Bishop Hugonin took a great liking to the girl and promised an answer after speaking with the Carmel superior. Saddened by the continued delay, Thérèse said, "I did more than *show my diamonds* to the Bishop. I *gave* him some!"

Appeal to the Pope

A few days later, Thérèse left with her father and sister Celine for a diocesan pilgrimage to Rome, which included a private audience with Pope Leo XIII. When the time came to meet the pontiff, the visitors were instructed not to speak as they received his individual blessing. Still, as she knelt down, Thérèse cried out, "Holy Father, I have a great favor to ask you! Permit me to enter Carmel at the age of fifteen!" After the priest on the pilgrimage explained that the matter was being considered by the Bishop, the Pope gazed at her and said, "Go, go. You will enter if God wills it!"

Thérèse wanted to say something more, but the guards touched her to make her rise. When she did not move, they took her by the arms and carried her out the door. A month later, Thérèse received her answer. She could enter Carmel after Lent—only three months away.

The "Little Way"

As Thérèse lived out her life in the monastery, the idea of her "little way" crystallized. She once explained to her sister that the way of spiritual childhood meant "to recognize one's nothingness, to expect everything from God, as a child expects everything from his father, to feel incapable of earning one's life, the eternal life of heaven."

A child *is* capable, however, of gathering flowers, and so Thérèse spent her life in gathering "flowers of sacrifice" to offer to the Lord. "Love is repaid by love alone," she wrote. In a myriad of small and unnoticed ways, Thérèse found opportunities to show her love for Jesus—by "not allowing one little sacrifice to escape, not one look, one word, profiting by all the smallest things and doing them through love."

For example, she made it a point to spend time with the

most disagreeable sisters, and to greet them with loving smiles. She would cut the bread for a disabled sister. She threw herself into prayer for foreign missionaries and adopted two spiritual "brothers"—priests to whom she wrote and encouraged in their missions. When appointed assistant novice mistress, she relied on God to help her to "feed the lambs" who were under her care. In all these situations, Thérèse felt she was fulfilling the vocation God had given to her—the call to love, a vocation which encompassed every other vocation in the church.

A Dark Night

Cold winters in unheated buildings and poor food eventually led to deteriorating health. Thérèse coughed up blood for the first time on Good Friday in 1896. At the same time, her soul was "invaded by the thickest darkness," and she began to wonder whether heaven was an illusion. However, few knew of this inner struggle. As she became weaker, she remained cheerful and serene.

On July 17, 1897, as she lay in the infirmary dying, Thérèse made her now famous prediction: "I feel that my mission is about to begin, my mission of making others love God as I love him, my mission of teaching my little way to souls. . . . I want to spend my heaven in doing good on earth." After her death, she said, she would "let fall a shower of roses."

Unable to breathe and suffering intensely, Thérèse died on September 30, 1897. Her autobiography was published and quickly became a spiritual classic. Stories circulated of the appearance of roses and their fragrance, along with miraculous healings and answers to prayers. She was can-onized in 1925 and in 1927, was made patroness of foreign missionaries. Her "little way" has become a road illuminated by the church for all to travel. In October 1997—one hun-dred years after her death—Pope John Paul II named Thérèse Martin a Doctor of the Church.

The "Little Way" to God

In her autobiography, *Story of a Soul*, St. Thérèse Martin writes of how she lived out her "little way"—her vocation to love others in the most ordinary of circumstances. This selection, which is addressed to the Mother Superior of her Carmelite monastery, was written in June 1897.

There is in the Community a Sister who has the faculty of displeasing me in everything, in her ways, her words, her character, everything seems *very disagreeable* to me. And still, she is a holy religious who must be very pleasing to God. Not wishing to give in to the natural antipathy I was experiencing, I told myself that charity must not consist in feelings but in works; then I set myself to doing for this Sister what I would do for the person I loved the most. Each time I met her I prayed to God for her, offering Him all her virtues and merits. I felt this was pleasing to Jesus, for there is no artist who doesn't love to receive praise for his works, and Jesus, the Artist of souls, is happy when we don't stop at the exterior, but, penetrating into the inner sanctuary where He chooses to dwell, we admire its beauty. I wasn't content simply with praying very much for this Sister who gave me so many struggles, but I took care to render her all the services possible, and when I was tempted to answer her back in a disagreeable manner, I was content with giving her my most friendly smile, and with changing the subject of the conversation, for the *Imitation [of Christ]* says: "It *is better to leave each one in his own opinion than to enter into arguments."*

Frequently, when I was at recreation (I mean during the work periods) and had occasion to work with this Sister, I used to run away like a deserter whenever my struggles became too violent. As she was absolutely unaware of my feelings for her, never did she suspect the motives for my conduct and she remained convinced that her character was very pleasing to me. One day at recreation she asked in almost these words: "Would you tell me, Sister Thérèse of the Child Jesus, what attracts you so much toward me; every time you look at me, I see you smile?" Ah! What attracted me was Jesus hidden in the depths of her soul; Jesus who makes sweet what is most bitter. I answered her that I was smiling because I was happy to see her (it is understood that I did not add that this was from a spiritual standpoint). . . .

Alas! when I think of the time of my novitiate I see how imperfect I was. I made so much fuss over such little things that it makes me laugh now. Ah! how good the Lord is in having matured my soul, and in having given it wings. All the nets of the hunters would not be able to frighten me, for: ". . .*the net is spread in vain before the eyes of them that have wings*" [Proverbs 1:17]. Later on, no doubt, the time in which I am now will appear filled with imperfections, but now I am astonished at nothing. I am not disturbed at seeing myself *weakness* itself. On the contrary, it is in my weakness that I glory [2 Corinthians 12:5], and I expect each day to discover new imperfections in myself. Remembering that *"charity covers a multitude of sins"* [Proverbs 10:12], I draw from this rich mine that Jesus has opened up before me.

The Lord, in the Gospel, explains in what *His new commandment* consists. He says in St. Matthew: *"You have heard that it was said, 'You shall love your neighbor and hate your enemy.' But I say to you, love your enemies . . . pray for those who persecute you"* [Matthew 5:43-44]. No doubt, we don't have any enemies in Carmel, but there are feelings. One feels attracted to this Sister, whereas with regard to another, one would make a long detour in order to avoid meeting her. And so, without even knowing it, she becomes the subject of persecution. Well, Jesus is telling me that it is this Sister who must be loved, she must be prayed for even though her conduct would lead me to believe that she doesn't love me.

The Life of Thérèse of Lisieux

1873 - Born on January 2 in Alençon to Zelie and Louis Martin

1877 - Thérèse's mother, Zelie, dies on August 28; family moves to Lisieux on November 15

1882 - Thérèse's sister Pauline enters the Carmel monastery in Lisieux

1883 - Falls seriously ill; recovers two months later

1886 - Thérèse's sister Marie enters Carmel monastery in Lisieux; Thérèse experiences grace of conversion on Christmas

1887 - *May 29*: Thérèse tells father of desire to become nun
October 31: Visits Bishop Hugonin in Bayeux for permission to enter Carmel
November 20: Audience with Pope Leo XIII

1888 - Enters Carmel on April 9

1890 - Makes profession on September 8

1894 - Thérèse's sister Celine enters Carmel

1895 - Begins to write her autobiography

1896 - Becomes novice mistress; spits up blood for the first time on Good Friday

1897 - Falls gravely ill in April and enters infirmary on July 8. Dies on September 30.

1898 - Thérèse's autobiography, *Story of a Soul*, is published

1899-1902 - First miracles and cures reported

1925 - Canonized on May 17 by Pope Pius XI

1927 - Declared patroness of foreign missionaries

1997 - Named Doctor of the Church by Pope John Paul II

I Have Called You by Name

Preacher to the Skeptics

Henri Lacordaire

1802 - 1861

The years surrounding the French Revolution were years of chaos. As France careened into disorder, its leaders jettisoned every practice and philosophy which could be remotely associated with the reviled monarchy, and that—in the minds and hearts of the populace—most certainly included the Catholic Church. Even the calendar was reconstructed, the years no longer being counted from the time of Christ's birth, but from the birth of the Revolution.

The high altar of Paris' Notre Dame Cathedral was desecrated by a mock sacrifice to the "Goddess of Reason." Churches were closed down, and religious orders disbanded. Their members who did not accept secularization either fled the country for safety or were expelled. Many priests and religious who remained but did not embrace the new regime were martyred. In every corner of the society, intellect and reason were enshrined above everything; God was considered irrelevant, if he existed at all.

Around the time that Henri Jean-Baptiste Lacordaire was born in 1802, the church was slowly coming out of its exile, but the road to restoration would be a long one. Local churches slowly began to reopen. Lacordaire's mother, Anne-Marie, widowed when Henri was only four years old, saw to the baptism and early catechesis of all four of her sons. The environment still remained decidedly unbelieving—especially among the younger generation. To Anne-Marie's dismay, none of her sons showed any real interest in the things of God, obedient and loyal to her though they were.

"Broad Daylight"

Lacordaire showed himself to be a brilliant student, and it was no surprise that he decided to study law in his ancestral home of Dijon. As successful as Lacordaire was at school, something continued to haunt him. The memory of his mother's lively faith and commitment to Christ remained with him no matter how far he claimed to have moved from the Catholicism of his youth. By the time he was practicing law in 1823, his friends often found him praying in the local church.

In his own words, he was experiencing a tension within himself, a tension between "cold, calm reason, opposed to a burning imagination. . . . I have a most religious heart and a very incredulous mind; but as it is in the nature of things that the mind must at last allow itself to be subjugated by the affections, it is most likely that I shall one day become a Christian." That day came not much later, and he described his experience in a letter to a friend: "I fancy I see a man grop-ing his way blindfolded; the bandage is gradually with-drawn; he has a glimmering of the daylight, and at the moment when the handkerchief falls he stands in the broad daylight."

The "broad daylight" in which Lacordaire found himself standing was so new that he began to reevaluate not only his career, but even the underlying philosophies and social structures of his time. As he observed the state of things in France and considered them in light of the gospel, Lacordaire became convinced that his country desperately needed the church to guide it in its quest for liberty, equality, and fra-ternity. The essential instinct of the people to seek social and political change was correct, but the philosophies and world view that drove many of the changes were wrong, and Lacordaire could see that. He saw that the push toward reform needed to be tempered by the teachings of Christ lest they fall prey to the subtle—and not-so-subtle—forces of atheism and rationalism.

Addressing a Siege Mentality

At a time when the church's intellectual and moral guid-ance was needed most, Lacordaire discovered a void. Even though bishops had once again taken up residence through-out the country, and parishes were reopening at an encour-aging rate, many of the church's leaders were caught up in a siege mentality. He observed:

What do the priests in the parishes do? They maintain the knowledge of Christian truths among women, a few men, a few youths. From time to time they withdraw from the environment of error a few souls, . . . and that is all. Shut up within their sanctuary . . . they are incapable of defending it from the attacks from outside. Sometimes they look down from the walls . . . and see that the besiegers have grown in numbers; making their way down to the interior of the Temple once more they tell what they have seen in sad and eloquent phrases which scarcely affect any save those who do not need to hear.

With a determination and abandon that characterized all his undertakings, Lacordaire decided to quit his profession, become a priest, and dedicate himself to filling this void in the church. He was a bit of a maverick in the seminary, questioning time-honored traditions in both theology and in practice, but because of his intellectual brilliance and depth in prayer and holiness, he was accepted and ordained to the priesthood in 1827.

Toward a Larger Role

Lacordaire's first few attempts at filling the gap were marked by turbulence, to say the least. In 1830, along with a fiery older priest, Abbé Félicité Robert de Lamennais, he undertook to publish a daily newspaper, *L'Avenir*. This paper's goal was to bring to public attention any action of the French government that might jeopardize the church's new-found and growing freedom. Lacordaire's articles were often direct attacks, either against the government, or against what he considered to be a weak and overly accommodating church.

The paper existed for a little more than a year, and Lacordaire made quite a name for himself—both good and bad, depending on one's predispositions. Those who opposed his sharp rhetoric and criticisms of the church's more conservative elements complained to the Pope. Consequently, the paper was silenced, and the two priests were ordered to bring their views into line. Lacordaire consented, but Lamennais refused, and ended up leaving not only the priesthood, but the church as well.

When *L'Avenir* was closed down, Lacordaire took a less prominent position within the Archdiocese of Paris, thus giving himself more time to pray and rest. This partial sabbatical was to be short-lived; his reputation as an energetic and intelligent man of God attracted the attention of other young, educated Catholics. They recognized in Lacordaire not only a sharp intellect but also a love for the church and a keen grasp of the philosophical and theological issues confronting Catholics of their day.

Accordingly, a number of them petitioned the Archbishop of Paris, asking him to allow Lacordaire to preach a series of sermons (or conferences) at Notre Dame Cathedral. They felt that their peers needed to hear the gospel preached in a way that would address the philosophies which had fueled the Revolution but had also given rise to atheistic rationalism. They were convinced that Lacordaire was their man.

After a good deal of hesitation, the bishop consented, permitting Lacordaire to preach without a prepared, preapproved text. This was a radical departure from the standard style of preaching, which was from prepared texts and which consisted more or less of a simple recitation of church doctrines and moral teachings. This format tended to produce very little creativity. As a result, it did not touch the younger generation whose minds were filled with popular philosophies but whose hearts were searching for something more permanent and trustworthy.

Every Sunday in the Lenten and Easter seasons of 1835, Notre Dame Cathedral was packed with people who had come to hear Lacordaire preach. He became so popular and effective that many arrived hours before the sermon, just hoping to get a seat! In his conferences, Lacordaire spoke about the nature of the church, its prophetic teaching, and the positive effects that Catholic doctrine should have upon both the individual and society.

In all his conferences, Lacordaire spoke with great respect for his listeners' quest for truth, for their intuitions about the limitations of the mind (despite its exaltation by modern philosophies), and about the fact that—in its teaching—the church holds out the promise of answers to even the deepest and most troubling of questions. He made no excuses for his disagreements with philosophies which denied the truth of the gospel; yet he did so in a way that was both respectful and compelling.

The Focus Shifts

As popular and respected as he was becoming, Lacordaire was not without his detractors. Many in the church distrusted him and accused him of siding too much with the liberal democracy of people like his old ally, Lamennais. Loyal to the old, monarchical way of the pre-Revolution church, they considered him—who had already been reprimanded by Rome once—a dangerous influence. Consequently, as Lacordaire's popularity grew, so did their complaints.

As the accusations and complaints about his preaching mounted, Lacordaire realized he could not continue on his present course. His own theological training was too limited to answer some of the objections, and many of his detractors were unrelenting. In April of 1836, before a stunned and saddened congregation, he announced his retirement from the pulpit. He returned to Rome to study theology and prayerfully reflect on his next step. He met with Pope Gregory XVI, as well as with a few cardinals, all of whom were warmly supportive and affectionate toward him despite the vehemence his name aroused in some quarters of the Vatican.

While in Rome, Lacordaire encountered a dimension of the church that he had never known before: "It seemed to me that since the destruction of the religious Orders [the church in France] had lost half her strength. I saw at Rome the magnificent remains of those institutions which had been founded by very great saints." He was impressed with the Benedictines, the Jesuits, and especially the Dominicans—the "Preaching Friars." These orders had all devoted themselves in one way or another to bringing the light of the gospel into the world, at the same time living apart from the world. As a result of such a life, the members of these orders were able to speak the truth to their contemporaries in ways that dealt with their needs and concerns and also raised their hearts and minds to consider things in the light of eternity.

Lacordaire felt that this was a necessity for France. He was only one man, able to preach from only one pulpit at a time. And even then he had encountered great opposition. But a religious order devoted to preaching—the Dominicans—that was another thing.

With characteristic single-mindedness, Lacordaire spent the next ten years working to reestablish the Dominican order in France, first entering the order himself in Rome and obtaining permission to establish foundations in France. He preached throughout the country, showing people what could happen when challenging, intelligent, and creative preaching took place. He preached conferences every year during the seasons of Advent, Lent and Easter. He dearly loved his new life, especially its combination of prayer, study, and active ministry. Here, in the most complete way, he was able to meet the needs of his time in an effective manner.

The Gospel of Freedom

After a brief, abortive attempt to enter politics and thus bring Catholicism more fully into the public square, Lacordaire retired permanently from public life to spend more time with his brother Dominicans. The Dominicans took over an ancient college in Sorèze, southwest of Toulouse, and in 1853 he took up teaching, a new role he embraced with excitement and vigor.

Lacordaire died on November 21, 1861, having spent his last few years in relative seclusion. To the end he remained an enigma to many people: How could a man with such progressive views call himself a faithful Catholic? Why, if he was so convinced about the way society should work, did he retire from it?

These questions not withstanding, there remains a prophetic element in Lacordaire's view of the world around him and its needs. It is true that he shared his countrymen's passion for liberty and democracy, yet he differed radically from most of his peers in his conviction that the liberty everyone sought could not possibly come about without the gospel. Rationalism without God exalted humanity beyond its proper limits. Eventually, rationalism declined to a radical subjectivism in which everyone was free to follow whatever his or her reason dictated. There was no room for absolute truth or the development of a common mind.

Lacordaire realized that any society devoid of shared values and beliefs could never be a truly free society. It could only devolve into a frustrating tension between individuals asserting their personal rights one against another. Without the preaching of the gospel—and a Christian understanding of the dignity of the person and the good of society—the quest for liberty would forever be stunted and frustrated. It was to this end that Lacordaire worked.

Preacher to the Skeptics

In one of his famous "conferences," Abbé Henri Jean-Baptiste Lacordaire argued that God has given human beings intuitive powers beyond that of pure reason.

By a look, single and simple, God sees all; he knows all, himself and all that which may spring from him, and when, from the high height of his eternal abode, he sees beforehand that which will some day happen, in myriads of centuries, his eye does not dilate; his eyebrow, more powerful than that of the Jupiter of Homer, does not move: He follows the succession and the change of created things by an immovable look.

Well, then! Why should we not be, to a certain degree, partakers of that supra-rational, supra-intelligible light—for we must create words to express these ideas, and, after all, I do not even create them—of that light, which is that of God? Why should not God, who has made man capable of seeing by principles and consequences, be able to distribute to him a certain degree of his own light for certain objects, and to a great end? Why should not man, who has the rational power of deduction and of induction, possess also the power of intuition? You possess that power, gentlemen, for so many things inferior to those which we are now considering. Intuition, that internal vision, beyond principles and consequences, is the very power of the human intelligence. Shall we give you some examples of this?

You all know presentiments; whether you adopt them or not it matters little, it is an historical fact; if you have not had them, I hope that you will have them some day. A presentiment—what is it? You are alone in your house—a feeling of sadness seizes upon you—you ask yourself why? You examine yourself; you are the same as you were before. Your affairs are in a good state; you are pleased with yourself, which is a thing too easy, and yet you are sad! Some days after, you hear that at the time of your sadness, without apparent cause, you were deprived of a friend—of a near relation: how did you know it? It is not by the course of principles and consequences, by inductions and deductions; you knew it by a secret and an inexplicable induction, by a light superior to that of logic.

You meet someone for the first time; you know nothing of his life, of his origin, his genesis, of his good or bad actions; you regarded him as Jesus Christ regarded the young man in the Gospel, of whom it is written: "*Looking on him, he loved him*" (Mark 10:21); you are touched by the soul expressed in that physiognomy; you love it; a sympathetic intuition places between you, in one single instant, that which logic would not have placed there in years. . . .

Shall not God have given us a divine intuition for this great work of life, a light which proceeds without composition or decomposition? For between rational light and mystic light there is the difference between the light which is decomposed in the prism, and a purer light, which could not be decomposed there.

Let us, then, again conclude, that since there exists a mystic certainty—that is to say, a conviction, unlearned,

transluminous, and which excludes doubt, there necessarily exists also a mystic power, or light, which is capable of producing that conviction.

The Life of Henri Lacordaire

1802 - Born on May 13 near Dijon, France

1806 - Father dies

1818-1822 - Studies law in Dijon and Paris; loses faith

1823 - Practices law; regains faith

1824 - Enters the seminary on May 12

1827 - Ordained on September 22

1830 - Begins collaboration with Abbé de Lamennais on newspaper, *L'Avenir*

1832 - Church condemns newspaper

1835 - Delivers first of his famous conferences at Notre Dame Cathedral in Paris

1836 - Announces intention of retiring from the world; goes to Rome and discovers the strength of the religious orders

1839 - Receives Dominican habit on April 9 in Rome

1840 - Makes vows on April 12 and returns to France

1843 - Establishes first house of restored Dominican order in Nancy, France; resumes conferences

1848 - Elected to French Assembly but resigns several months later

1853 - Gives up conferences; teaches at military school of Sorèze, southwest of Toulouse

1861 - Dies on November 21

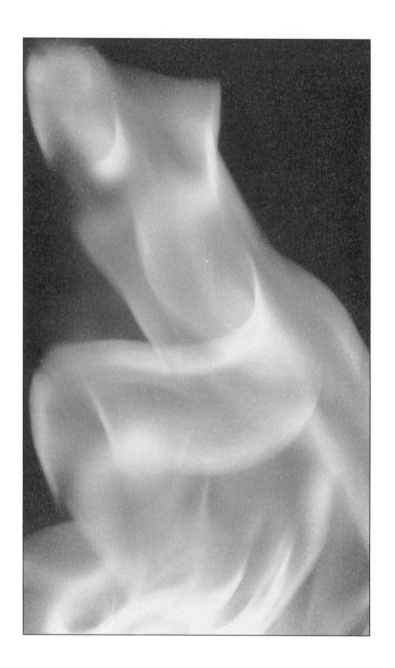

Portrait of a Martyr

Saint Ignatius of Antioch

37 - 107

*May nothing seen or unseen begrudge me making
my way to Jesus Christ. Come, fire, cross, battling with wild
beasts, wrenching of bones, mangling of limbs,
crushing of my whole body, cruel tortures of the devil—
only let me get to Jesus Christ.*
(Ignatius of Antioch, Letter to the Romans)

Ignatius Theophorus, bishop of Antioch, was an old man when he reached the Roman arena in the winter of the year 107. He had made an arduous journey by land and sea, accompanied by ten brutal guards whom he referred to as "leopards." To the assembled crowds, he was just another fanatical Christian who refused to venerate the Roman gods and emperor. His wish for a quick end was granted: Two hungry lions quickly tore him to pieces. The crowds cheered, their perverse fascination with gore and blood satisfied. It was said that only two large bones remained of him.

Martyrdom, of course, was no rare occurrence in ancient Rome at the dawn of Christianity. When one became a Christian, he or she knew full well that the consequences might be a horrible death. The martyrdom of Ignatius, however, and his long journey to Rome, stand out because they were memorialized in the seven passionate letters he wrote to Christian communities along the way.

Today, when pain and suffering are often viewed as the ultimate enemies, Ignatius' earnest desire to face the lions can be especially incomprehensible to us. However, Ignatius was no masochist. His desire to suffer and die for the Lord was born of a faith so strong that he saw eternal life as more of a reality than life on earth. For him, death was a celebration of rebirth.

Loving the Body of Christ

Little is known about Ignatius other than what we can glean from his letters. He may have been Jewish, Greek, or Syrian. According to legend, he was the little child Jesus held in his lap in Capernaum (Matthew 18:2). Ignatius was the Bishop of Antioch in Syria, the third most important city in the Roman empire at the time. As a young man, he probably knew the apostles Peter and John, and his letters quote passages from Paul's epistles.

Ignatius' writings reveal a man who loved the infant church deeply and sought to keep her from the heresies threatening the truth. Amazingly, nearly two thousand years later, the truth described by Ignatius has been preserved by the church. The window on early Christianity we glimpse through his letters shows us a church that is clearly recognizable as our own.

The church over which Ignatius presided had suffered waves of persecution, depending on the attitude of the emperor in power. These persecutions were sparked by the refusal of Christians to worship pagan idols. Romans were required to publicly venerate the gods. Those refusing to participate in ceremonial veneration—which involved burning a few grains of incense before a statue—risked angering the gods and thus jeopardizing the welfare of the state. The government cared little about the other religions in the empire, as long as the people participated in a mass appeasement of Apollo, Jupiter, Mars and other popular deities.

The Danger of Being Different

Roman officials were infuriated by the stubborn refusal of most Christians to worship the gods. It did not help that those professing faith in Christ were out of the mainstream for other reasons too. They did not participate in the rampant immorality that was acceptable to most Romans. They would not eat meat slaughtered by pagans when the animals had been sacrificed to the gods. They avoided the popular "games" in the arena and refused to celebrate the emperor's birthday because the Romans considered him a god. Rumors about their celebration of the Eucharist abounded. Some said they ate real flesh and blood.

Ironically, however, it was under an emperor considered competent and just that Ignatius was murdered. A respected military commander, Trajan became emperor in 98. He did not hunt out Christians; if a public complaint was lodged against a Christian, that person was given the opportunity to refute the charge by offering prayers to the idols. In 107, traveling through Antioch, Trajan heard complaints about the large Christian community there, and sent for their leader, Bishop Ignatius. Here is an account of the conversation that took place between the two men:

Trajan: "Who are you, spirit of evil, who dare to disobey my orders and who goad others on to their destruction?"

Ignatius: "No one calls Theophorus spirit of evil."

Trajan: "Who is Theophorus?"

Ignatius: "He who bears Christ within him."

Trajan: "And we—do we not bear within ourselves these gods who help us against our enemies?"

Ignatius: "No. You are wrong when you call gods those who are no better than devils. There is only one God who made heaven and earth and all that is in them, and one Jesus Christ into whose Kingdom I earnestly desire to be admitted."

Trajan: "Do you mean him who was crucified under Pontius Pilate?"

Ignatius: "Yes, the same who by his death has crucified both sin and its author, and has proclaimed that every malice of the devil should be trodden under foot by those who bear him in their hearts."

Trajan: "Do you then carry Christ about within you?"

Ignatius: "Yes, for it is written, 'I will dwell in them and will walk with them.' "

A Journey Toward Life

Trajan ordered Ignatius to be bound and sent to Rome to face death. The bishop was said to have thanked God for the privilege of following St. Paul in chains. Thus began his long journey with the "ten leopards" who, according to Ignatius, "only become worse under the influence of kindness—I fight it out with beasts from Syria to Rome by land and by sea, day and night."

Ignatius became a celebrity in chains. At each stop, the faithful would line the streets for his blessing. Even as he marched to his death, Ignatius, through the letters he dispatched along the way, exhibited an overriding concern that the faithful not be misled by heresy. He encouraged the communities to be obedient to their pastoral leaders in all things. He also assailed those who "refuse to admit that the Eucharist is the flesh of our Savior, Jesus Christ," and added: "You should regard that Eucharist as valid which is celebrated either by the bishop or by someone he authorizes."

The most striking letter, however, is the one Ignatius wrote to the church in Rome, in which he asked his fellow Christians not to make any efforts to prevent his martyrdom:

I plead with you, do not do me an unseasonable kindness. Let me be fodder for wild beasts—that is how I can get to God. I am God's wheat and I am being ground by the teeth of wild beasts to make a pure loaf for Christ. I would rather that you fawn on the beasts so that they may be my tomb and no scrap of my body be left. Thus, when I have fallen asleep, I shall be a burden to no one. Then I shall be a real disciple of Jesus Christ when the world sees my body no more. Pray Christ for me that by these means I may become God's sacrifice.

In one section of this letter, we get a glimpse into Ignatius' all-consuming desire to be martyred:

Do not talk Jesus Christ and set your hearts on the

world. . . . For though alive, it is with a passion for death that I am writing to you. My Desire has been crucified and there burns in me no passion for material things. There is living water in me, which speaks and says inside me, "Come to the Father." I take no delight in corruptible food or in the dainties of this life. What I want is God's bread, which is the flesh of Christ, who came from David's line; and the drink I want, his blood: an immortal love feast indeed!

As Ignatius was led into the arena with its cheering crowds, the lions approached. His last words were, "May I have joy of these wild beasts." St. John Chrysostom said that as the bishop's few remains were brought back to Antioch, "the cities . . . escorted the crowned one with praises, celebrating the champion in song; laughing the Devil to scorn." In 637, just before Antioch was overtaken by the Saracens, Ignatius' relics were transferred to the Church of St. Clement of Rome.

Chrysostom also said that Ignatius demonstrated the power of the resurrected Christ:

For in reality it is the greatest proof of the resurrection that the slain Christ should show forth so great power after death, as to persuade living men to despise both country and home and friends, and acquaintance and life itself, for the sake of confessing him, and to choose in place of present pleasures, both stripes and dangers and death.

Portrait of a Martyr

This letter by St. Ignatius was written
to the Christians at Tralles, a town in Asia
Minor. The church community there had sent
their bishop, Polybius, to greet Ignatius while
he stopped in Smyrna on his way to Rome to
be martyred.

Full hearty greetings in apostolic style, and every good wish from Ignatius, the "God-inspired," to the holy church at Tralles in Asia. You are dear to God, the Father of Jesus Christ, elect and a real credit to him, being completely at peace by reason of the Passion of Jesus Christ, who is our Hope, since we shall rise in union with him.

Well do I realize what a character you have—above reproach and steady under strain. It is not just affected, but it comes naturally to you, as I gathered from Polybius, your bishop. By God's will and that of Jesus Christ, he came to me in Smyrna, and so heartily congratulated me on being a prisoner for Jesus Christ that in him I saw your whole congregation. I welcomed, then, your godly good will, which reached me by him, and I gave thanks that I found you, as I heard, to be following God. . . .

In your bishop I received the very model of your love, and I have him with me. His very bearing is a great lesson, while his gentleness is most forceful. I imagine even the godless respect him.

While I could write about this matter more sharply, I spare you out of love. Since, too, I am a convict, I have not thought it my place to give you orders like an apostle. God has granted me many an inspiration, but I keep my limits, lest boasting should be my undoing. For what I need most at this point is to be on my guard and not to heed flatterers. Those who tell me . . . they are my scourge. To be sure, I am ever so eager to be a martyr, but I do not know if I deserve to be. Many people have no notion of my impetuous ambition. Yet it is all the more a struggle for me. What I need is gentleness by which the prince of this world is overthrown. . . .

Be deaf . . . to any talk that ignores Jesus Christ, of David's lineage, of Mary; who was really born, ate, drank; was really persecuted under Pontius Pilate; was really crucified and died, in the sight of heaven and earth and the underworld. He was really raised from the dead, for his Father raised him, just as his Father will raise us, who believe on him, through Christ Jesus, apart from which we have no genuine life.

And if, as some atheists (I mean unbelievers) say, his suffering was a sham (it's really they who are a sham!), why, then, am I a prisoner? Why do I want to fight with wild beasts? In that case I shall die to no purpose. Yes, and I am maligning the Lord too! . . .

From Smyrna I send you my greetings in which the churches of God that are here with me join. They have altogether raised my spirits—yes, completely. My very chains which I carry around for Jesus Christ's sake, in my desire to get to God, exhort you, "Stay united and pray for one another!". . .

The Smyrnaeans and Ephesians send their greetings with love. Remember the church of Syria in your prayers. I am not worthy to be a member of it: I am the least of their number. Farewell in Jesus Christ. Submit to the bishop as to [God's] law, and to the presbytery too. All of you, love one another with an undivided heart. My life is given for you, not only now but especially when I shall get to God. I am still in danger. But the Father is faithful: he will answer my prayer and yours because of Jesus Christ. Under his influence may you prove to be spotless.

The Life of Ignatius of Antioch

c. 37 - Born in Syria

c. 69 - Named Bishop of Antioch, third most important city in the Roman empire

98 - Trajan becomes emperor of Roman Empire

107 - Arrested by Trajan and sent to Rome bound in chains. Arrives in Rome on December 20 and is killed by lions in the arena

637 - Before Antioch is overtaken by the Saracens, Ignatius' relics are transferred to the Church of St. Clement in Rome

I Have Called You by Name

God's Gracious Warrior

Saint Joan of Arc

1412 - 1431

Dressed in full armor, with a red and gold cloak over her shoulders, Joan the Maid stood proudly next to her King in the cathedral in Rheims. The Dauphin Charles—eldest son of the deceased King Charles VI—had returned to claim his crown. Although the English still controlled most of northern France, Charles had reasserted his right to rule his country—a right that had been taken from him by a treaty his father was forced to sign ten years before. The coronation would be the turning point in a struggle with the English that had lasted nearly one hundred years.

Joan, a seventeen-year-old peasant girl from the small town of Domremy, gave Charles the victory by leading the French army into battle. Exhibiting military prowess and expertise which belied her years and experience, Joan was the visible symbol of hope and courage to a flagging army and a faint-hearted king.

Strange Voices

How could a young, inexperienced village girl accomplish what kings and army commanders had failed to do? At least part of the answer was to be found in Joan herself. She was bold and courageous, single-minded, and strong—all traits which were born of an unwavering faith in God. She never doubted that the voices she began hearing at age thirteen, and which continued until her death at nineteen, were from the Lord and would enable her to succeed in the great mission to which she had been called.

The voices came suddenly one day to the pious girl, who could neither read nor write and spent her time spinning and watching over the livestock. At the time, she told no one, even after the voices became visions of St. Catherine, St. Margaret, and St. Michael the Archangel. They became more insistent that she begin her task.

The voices were specific. She must go to the nearby town of Vaucouleurs to meet with the Governor, Robert de Baudicourt, to ask him to bring her to the Dauphin. When she was sixteen—without telling her parents what she was up to—Joan asked her cousin to take her to Vaucouleurs. The governor only laughed when she told him she had been called by God to save France. Discouraged but not defeated, Joan returned several months later, ostensibly to help a relative care for a new baby. This time, two young knights became intrigued with Joan and agreed to help. Baudicourt relented. In the winter of 1429, dressed in men's clothing for protection on the long and perilous trip, Joan set off on horseback with the two knights to the king's castle in Chinon.

"I Am Joan the Maid."

More than three hundred people of the royal court were in the great hall of the castle as Joan entered. The Dauphin had purposely dressed down for the occasion to hide his identity from the girl, but she recognized him immediately and knelt before him. "Gentle Dauphin, I am Joan the Maid. The King of Heaven sends me with this message. You shall be crowned in Rheims, and I will raise the siege of Orleans, for it is God's will that the English shall leave France." He took her aside for a private conversation. Whatever she told him impressed him so much that witnesses said his face was radiant when they returned to the hall.

Still, Charles was cautious. He sent Joan to Poiters to be grilled for several weeks by theologians to see if she could be trusted. Joan—impatient with the delay—was neither overawed nor particularly submissive to her questioners. When asked by one churchman what dialect her voices used, she answered, "Better than yours." Asked if she believed in God, she snapped, "Better than you do."

She passed the test and was sent to be fitted for armor. A banner was made according to Joan's specifications. As for her sword, she asked the priests at St. Catherine's Chapel in Fierbois—a town along the way to Chinon—to search behind the altar. They were astonished to discover an old rusty sword which was subsequently polished and presented to Joan. Although she cherished her sword, she said later she loved her banner "forty times better." By holding it up in battle, she said, she had avoided killing anyone with her own hands.

Fighting for Her King

Her first objective was to liberate the city of Orleans, which had been under siege by the English for months and whose takeover would bring the English across the Loire River into territory loyal to the Dauphin. On April 29, 1429, Joan and several thousand soldiers arrived in Orleans, bringing needed supplies. Although she was not the official commander, she prohibited unmarried female companions from accompanying the soldiers and insisted that the men go to confession. Traveling with her own personal confessor, Joan heard Mass whenever possible.

Joan insisted on warning the English before the battle began; she was answered with cruel insults that made her cry. In the first few days of fighting, the French were able to overrun a number of smaller English forts stationed outside the city. Joan's first experience in battle was a shock, and she wept when she saw either English or French soldiers dying. At one point, she dismounted her horse to comfort a dying Englishman.

On May 7, Joan—who had predicted that she would be wounded—was struck by an arrow. She wept from the pain of the six-inch wound, and was taken to be bandaged. She returned to find the French retreating, but when they saw her standard, they rallied and charged the fort of Les Tourelles again. The English ran back across a burning drawbridge, fell into the river and drowned. The people of Orleans rejoiced; Joan was their angel from God.

Joan's next goal was to have the Dauphin crowned in Rheims, the traditional city for French coronations. This meant capturing English strongholds in the Loire Valley along the way. The momentum was with Joan and her army. After a major victory at Patay, they quickly captured several other important towns and made their way to Rheims. Charles VII was crowned on July 17, 1429. "Gentle King," Joan said in tears as she embraced his knees: "Now is done God's pleasure."

Betrayal and Capture

Instead of allowing Joan to lead the campaign to take Paris, Charles was duped into signing a treaty with the Duke of Burgundy, who was allied with the English. This gave the enemy more time to assemble troops and provisions. Finally, Charles was persuaded to attack Paris, but the momentum had been lost. The first two attempts failed.

Joan's voices warned her that she would soon be captured, and on May 23, 1430, during a skirmish in Compiegne, soldiers of the Duke of Burgundy surrounded her. The king made no effort to rescue her or pay her ransom, but she never spoke a word against him. Held in a castle by an overlord of the Duke, Joan attempted to escape by jumping from the roof of a sixty-foot tower. She miraculously survived. Finally, she was sold to the English, transported to a prison in Rouen, and secured in heavy chains because she refused to promise that she would not try to escape again.

Bishop Pierre Cauchon, in whose diocese Joan had been captured, presided at a church trial that attempted to prove that the young virgin from Lorraine was a heretic and a witch. Cauchon, who sided with the English, called nearly sixty canon lawyers and doctors of the church, most of whom were as anxious as he to smear the reputations of both Joan and her king. The trial was rigged; she was provided no lawyer; the records of the trial were tampered with; and anyone disagreeing with Cauchon's tactics was threatened.

Still, Joan's intelligent and quick answers disarmed her prosecutors. For example, when asked if St. Michael had appeared to her wearing clothing, she replied, "Do you think our Lord has nothing to dress him in?" Questioned whether St. Margaret spoke the English language, she answered, "How should she speak English since she is not on the side of the English?" The inquisitors were especially concerned that Joan refused to wear female attire. When asked whether she thought she was in a state of grace, Joan answered: "If I am not, may God bring me to it; If I am, may God keep me in it."

Frail, but Steadfast

The question eventually boiled down to one: Would Joan, in submission to the church, agree that her voices were diabolical or illusions? She was even threatened with torture, to no avail. In the end, she was pronounced guilty. On May 24, 1431, as the Bishop read out her sentence, she broke down and recanted, agreeing to defer to the church.

It was the fear of being burned that led to the recantation. Several days later, Joan was again in male dress and declared once more that her voices were from God. Through these voices, she said, God had told her that by saving her life, she would be damning herself. She was now ready to face death. On May 30, she was led to a high scaffold. A paper cap on her head read, "Heretic, relapsed, apostate, idolatress." She asked to look at a crucifix.

As the flames rose around her, her last words were,

"Jesus, Jesus." Many wept, and one English official remarked: "We are lost; we have burnt a saint!" The executioner had been ordered to gather up Joan's ashes and throw them into the Seine, but despite all his efforts, he could not get her heart to burn.

The French armies eventually pushed the English out of France. Twenty years later, King Charles ordered a new trial, and Joan was declared innocent. In 1920, Joan of Arc—already a saint in the eyes of the French—was canonized by the church that had once excommunicated her. Joan's remarkable story has been told many times and her courage applauded even by nonbelievers. For Christians, however, she remains a symbol of hope: Frail as we are, if we allow ourselves to be used for God's purposes, we can accomplish the impossible.

God's Gracious Warrior

St. Joan was interrogated from January through March, 1431. The following selection was taken from the text of one day's questioning on March 17. Master Jean de La Fontaine had been charged by Bishop Pierre Cauchon to question Joan.

La Fontaine: In what form, size, appearance and clothing does St. Michael come to you?

Joan: He was in the form of a true and honest man, and as for the clothes and other things, I shall not tell you any more. As for the angels, I saw them with my own eyes and you will get no more out of me about that. I believe as firmly the doings and sayings of St. Michael who appeared to me as I believe that our Lord Jesus Christ suffered death and passion for us. And what moves me to believe this is the good advice, the good comfort and the good doctrine that he did and gave me.

La Fontaine: Will you leave to the determination of our Holy Mother the Church, all your matters whether in good or in evil?

Joan: As for the Church, I love her and would wish to sustain her with all my power for our Christian faith. And it is not I who should be prevented from going to church and hearing Mass. As for the good works which I have done and at my coming, I must put my faith in the King of Heaven, who sent me to Charles, son of Charles, King of France, who is King of France. And you will see that the French will soon win a great thing which God will send to these French, such that it will rock the whole kingdom of France. I say it that when it happens you may remember that I said it.

La Fontaine: After how long will this happen?

Joan: In Our Lord's own time.

La Fontaine: Will you abide by the Church's determination for your sayings and deeds?

Joan: I abide by God who sent me, by the Holy Virgin and all the saints in paradise. And I am of opinion that it is all one and the same thing, God and the Church, and that of that one should make no difficulty. Why do you make difficulty over that?

La Fontaine: There is a Church Triumphant where are God, the saints, the angels and souls already saved. And there is the Church Militant in which are the Pope, God's vicar on earth, the cardinals and prelates of the Church, the clergy, and all good Christians and Catholics. This well-composed Church cannot err and is ruled by the Holy Spirit. That is why I ask you whether you are willing to abide by (put your trust in) the Church Militant, that is to say, the one which is on earth, as I have explained to you.

Joan: I went to the King of France from God and the Virgin Mary and all the saints in paradise and the Church Victorious above and by their commandment. And to that Church I submit all my good deeds and all that I have done and shall do. As for submitting myself to the Church Militant, I shall answer you nothing else for the time being. . . .

La Fontaine: Since you have said that you would wear woman's clothes if you were allowed to go away, would that please God?

Joan: If permission were given me to withdraw in woman's clothes, immediately (thereafter) I should dress in man's clothes, and do what is commanded me by God; and

I have answered elsewhere that not for anything whatsoever would I take oath not to put on armor and not to wear man's clothes to do the Lord's commandment.

La Fontaine: What ages (are), and what garments are worn by, Saints Catherine and Margaret?

Joan: To that you shall have the answer you have already had from me and none other. I have answered as most certainly as I know. . . .

La Fontaine: Do you know whether Saints Catherine and Margaret hate the English?

Joan: They love that which God loves and hate that which God hates.

La Fontaine: Does God hate the English?

Joan: Of the love or hate which God has for the English and of what he does to their souls, I know nothing; but well I know that they will be driven out of France, excepting those who will die there, and that God will send victory to the French over the English.

La Fontaine: Was God for the English when their cause was prospering in France?

Joan: I know not if God hated the French, but I believe that it was his will to let them be stricken for their sins if there were sins among them.

La Fontaine: What guarantee and what succor do you expect from God for your wearing of man's clothes?

Joan: For the clothes as for the other things I have done, I expect no other recompense than the salvation of my soul.

The Life of Joan of Arc

1412 - Born in January in the small village of Domremy

1425 - Begins hearing voices

1428 - Asks her cousin to take her to Vaucouleurs to meet
with the governor, who dismisses her

1429 - *January:* Goes again to Vaucouleurs, and with aid
of two knights, convinces governor to allow her to
meet the Dauphin
February 23: Sets off to Chinon with the two
knights to see the Dauphin
April 29: Arrives in Orleans with several thousand
soldiers
May 7: Injured in battle but leads victorious
charge against the English
July 17: Dauphin is crowned Charles VII in
Rheims
September 8: Attack on Paris fails

1430 - Captured by Duke of Burgundy on May 23; kept
in tower of castle in Rouen

1431 - *January 9:* Trial begins with Bishop Pierre Cauchon
presiding
May 24: Breaks down and recants as sentence is
read
May 28: Reasserts that voices were from God
May 30: Burned at the stake by the English

1456 - Rehabilitation trial ends in revocation of sentence

1920 - Joan is canonized by Pope Benedict XV

Tested by Fire

Blessed Mary MacKillop
1842 - 1909

Mary MacKillop remained calm—almost serene—as the bishop pronounced the words that would separate her from her church. A twenty-nine-year-old Australian woman who had started a religious order dedicated to teaching poor children, Mary knew she was being excommunicated unjustly by the bishop. At a moment when she might have drowned in despair, however, Mary felt "nearer to God than I had ever felt before."

It was neither the first nor the last trial that Blessed Mary MacKillop would endure. Born on January 15, 1842 in Melbourne, Australia, Mary was the oldest child of Scottish immigrants. Her father, Alexander, a one-time seminarian, was known for his impulsive business dealings. Consequently, the family moved often and would frequently have to live off the charity of relatives. This instability made home life difficult, as Mary herself confessed: "My life as a child was one of sorrow, my home when I had it, a most unhappy one."

The First Stirrings

A beautiful child with deep-set eyes that revealed an intelligence and maturity far beyond her years, Mary absorbed all that her father taught her about the gospel. As the oldest child, she felt a strong sense of duty to help care for her family. At the age of sixteen, she began working to help support them.

In 1860, when she was eighteen, Mary left Melbourne for Penola in South Australia to earn money as a governess for her aunt and uncle. Penola was a small town surrounded by the Australian bush, where poor shepherds and miners lived in primitive conditions and struggled to feed their families. In this remote corner, Mary met Father Julian Woods, a parish priest who had been thinking of founding an order of sisters to teach poor Catholic children about their faith.

When Mary confided in him her desire to live a religious life and serve the poor, Woods believed God had sent her. Together they dreamed of opening a Catholic school in Penola. But it wasn't until six years later—when some of Mary's younger siblings were old enough to help with the family finances—that their dream became a reality. Housed in a stable, the first Catholic school in Penola opened, accepting money only from those families who could afford to pay.

Several women joined Mary and with her, they became the first members of the Institute of St. Joseph of the Sacred Heart. The success of this first school led quickly to the opening of a second thirty miles away, and in 1867, Mary left for Adelaide with another sister to open even more schools.

Sharing in Poverty

The growth of the order was rapid: Within three years, seventy-two sisters were teaching in twenty-one schools and running an orphanage and a refuge for homeless women. Despite the demands that such responsibilities placed on her,

Mary would frequently spend many hours of the night in prayer and worship.

Mary also worked hard to communicate her vision of the order to the women who joined her. "Let others seek the better, more remarkable places, but let St. Joseph's true children . . . seek first the poorest, most neglected parts of God's vineyard," she told them. Their nourishment and joy would come from the Blessed Sacrament. True to this vision, the sisters lived in the same poverty as those they served—especially in the outback, where luxuries were unknown. One convent, for example, had no lighting, and because there was no fuel for a fire, the sisters survived on raw cabbage.

Mary was known for her extreme kindness to her sisters. She did all she could to make sure they had at least the basic necessities, even to the point of begging in the streets to support the work. Some were offended by the begging and criticized her for accepting unsuitable candidates who could not handle the grueling lifestyle. However, the Bishop of Adelaide, Lawrence Sheil, remained enthusiastic and approved a rule governing the order written by Woods.

In 1870, at the request of the bishop there, Mary went to Queensland to open more schools. Catholic as well as Anglican schools in the diocese were entitled to government funding on the condition that Christian formation be kept to a minimum. Even though he knew that accepting the funds and limiting their efforts at evangelization violated the sisters' rule, Bishop James Quinn hoped that they would take the money and that Mary would not oppose him.

It would not be the first time a bishop miscalculated Mary's resolve to stand up for the calling God had given her and the Institute. "It is *impossible* for us to become in any way connected with Government and be true to . . . our Rule," Mary wrote. Josephite schools—without government money—soon opened in the diocese.

A New Threat

While in Queensland, Mary became alarmed at reports coming from Adelaide. Father Woods and two sisters were claiming to experience supernatural visions and diabolical visitations. What was worse, even after the sisters later confessed that they were lying, Woods continued to believe their stories. Although Mary was bound to accept the direction of Woods, she became increasingly concerned and anxious about his ability to guide the Institute.

When Bishop Sheil returned to Adelaide from Europe in 1871, he was presented with a written complaint against the Josephites from half of the priests in his diocese, many of whom were annoyed by Woods and his odd stories. But the complaint didn't come from completely pure motives. Charles Horan, a trusted advisor of Sheil's, had written the complaint because he wanted to take revenge on Woods for reporting the scandalous conduct of one of his friends. Nevertheless, Sheil announced that the sisters would have to accept changes to their rule: The order was to be placed under the authority of the bishop. The sisters would no longer be free to govern themselves.

Mary acknowledged the bishop's right to change a rule he had originally approved. But since the sisters had taken vows to the original rule, she insisted that they had a right to decide whether to leave the diocese and stay with the Institute, or to take vows to the new rule and become part of a diocesan group. Refusing to meet with Mary, Sheil ordered her to leave immediately for a convent fifty miles away, but she delayed the trip until she could speak to him about his decision.

The next day—September 22, 1871—Bishop Sheil went to the Adelaide convent and summoned Mary. He then excommunicated her for disobeying his orders. "I must at least try not to abuse God's love by speaking ill of—or making known the faults of—his servants," Mary wrote in one letter during this time. Nearby Jesuits, who considered the excommunication invalid, continued to give her Communion.

On his deathbed six months later, Bishop Sheil realized that Horan had deceived him and sought to make amends. He lifted the excommunication and appointed an episcopal commission to exonerate Mary. He also replaced Woods—who continued to cause problems—as director of the Institute. For the remainder of his life, Woods rebuffed Mary's attempts to continue their friendship.

The excommunication episode made it clear that the Josephites needed the protection of Rome. So, in 1873, Mary traveled to the Vatican to seek approval for her rule. While the Holy See found the rule confusing, it did write a provisional rule which permitted the institute to continue to be run by a superior general and not by the diocesan bishops.

Oil on Troubled Waters

But Mary's trials were far from over. Brisbane's bishop, James Quinn, and his brother in Bathurst, Bishop Matthew Quinn, both wanted to run the order themselves in their own dioceses. In both cases, she was forced to withdraw her sisters.

Mary's actions were backed by Rome, but Mary had to endure James Quinn accusing her of ambition and stubbornness and calling her the daughter of a bankrupt seminarian.

Mary wrote, "I often feel inclined to envy my quiet country sisters who have the same daily routine and so much peace whilst I am one day in a rough mail coach, again in a steamer, in rain and storm, but worse than all, when I have to see bishops and priests, and, in the cause of our loved work, have to hold out against all their arguments and threats."

Amid these struggles, Mary continued her travels across Australia and into New Zealand, where she visited her order's many schools and convents and encouraged the women who had chosen to serve God in such a selfless way. "Anyone who would go to Mother in trouble would tell you that they felt better after," said one sister. "She seemed to be able to throw oil on troubled waters."

Mary's last major struggle was with a former friend of the Institute. Bishop Christopher Reynolds of Adelaide—who succeeded Sheil—began to blame some of the diocese's monetary problems on the Josephites. He accused Mary of drinking and embezzlement. While her doctor had prescribed a tablespoon of brandy before each meal for health reasons, Mary had always insisted that another sister administer it. Still, she was found guilty and expelled from the diocese. When she realized that the inquiry had been conducted unfairly and without the knowledge of the Holy See—even though Reynolds had told her otherwise—Mary could only say, "God's ways are most mysterious."

From Adelaide, Mary went to Sydney, where the bishop there welcomed her, but the affair had taken its toll on her:

"I now feel the effects of years of care and anxiety. It seemed only to require this quarrel with the Bishop I loved to make me *almost* completely break down. I say *almost* for I am trying hard for my Sisters' sake to keep up."

In 1888, the patience of the sisters was rewarded. The Holy See confirmed the central government of the Institute. Mary continued to serve the Lord with her whole heart and soul, even after a debilitating stroke in 1902. She died peacefully on August 9, 1909, at the motherhouse in Sydney. The process for her canonization was delayed more than twenty years by the allegations made by Bishop Reynolds, but was taken up again in 1951. On January 19, 1995, Mary MacKillop was beatified by Pope John Paul II. Today, thirteen hundred Sisters of St. Joseph are serving the Lord in schools, hospitals and welfare agencies throughout Australia, New Zealand, and Peru.

Tested by Fire

Bl. Mary MacKillop's order, the Sisters of
St. Joseph of the Sacred Heart, had established
eight houses in New Zealand when she visited
the island. In this letter, dated August 8, 1894,
she described what it was like for the nuns to
live in the house in Matata.

I must give you some idea of what Matata is like. Imagine
a big straggling barn, but a two storyed one. On the ground
floor we have entrance hall, reception room, and a large
school—used as a chapel on Sundays, holy days and festivals.
. . . There are besides, downstairs, a sort of passage used for
laundry work and a lumber room. Upstairs we have a *very nice
oratory* with matting on the floor. We have our dear Lord
always with us, and Mass is daily said by one of the Fathers.

Off the top landing a door leads to the kitchen, which is
simply a passage fifteen feet long by six feet wide. At the end,
opposite the door, there is a miserable stove with which cooking is done. Off this kitchen is a little closet used as a refec-
tory—eight feet by six. A board two feet wide and about five
feet long is fixed against the outer partition and this serves
as a table. Shelves above this contain the crockery in use,
knives, spoons, etc. All is very neat and clean. In fine
weather it is all right, but when rain and wind come, the first
pours in all directions, and the second causes the whole place
to shake and the fire to smoke. Indeed, at such times, to keep
this fire alight and do any necessary cooking, Sister Genevieve
has to stand in water—and for the purpose wears strong
leather boots.

Just imagine how cold this [the community room] must be in winter. From the floor to the highest beam in the roof there must be a height of twenty feet, and *there is no fireplace anywhere in the house*—not even in the kitchen which has only a miserable stove. . . . On the coldest mornings and during the day, all have to work and exercise themselves to keep warm. The cold is very much felt during school hours, but so far has had to be endured. Please God, this will be remedied next year, for when I return to Auckland I shall, God willing, not leave a stone unturned to procure a stove for the community room, school and kitchen.

The food is the poorest; meat very seldom, once in a month perhaps—fish just as the Maoris please to get them any, wild duck, swans, or wild pig, whenever any of the fathers succeed in shooting or killing such. It is often a feast or a famine here. The chief food is the sweet potato. Butter and milk are luxuries for which they pay dearly and which they can only procure from one person.

The Maoris sing the Vespers through themselves in their own language, but the Litany and hymns for Benediction they sing in Latin. The Vespers were originally taught to the Maoris by Bishop Pompallier about seventy years ago, and the old Maoris of that time in their turn taught their children. This is an important thing to remember, as they were a long time without priests, for, between wars and changes in the Auckland diocese, the poor Maoris had little to remind them of their religion.

From the community room and balcony we have a lovely view. From where I sit writing this, there is a view of the ocean and several small islands—one being "White Island" which contains an active volcano, which is smoking away at present at a great rate. Looking towards the south east there is a range of hills—can hardly call them mountains. Between the Convent and the sea, just about five minutes walk from here, is a fresh water creek running parallel with it and only separated from it by a sandy ridge, not many yards wide. This is a lovely day, and everything looks bright and beautiful.

The Life of Mary MacKillop

1842 - Born on January 15 in Melbourne, Australia

1860 - Arrives in Penola in South Australia to earn money as a governess; meets Father Julian Woods

1866 - With Father Woods, establishes Catholic school in Penola for poor children; Sisters of St. Joseph formed

1867 - Moves to Adelaide to establish more schools; Josephite order grows rapidly

1870 - At request of the bishop, Mary opens more schools in Queensland

1871 - Bishop of Adelaide, Lawrence Sheil, excommunicates Mary on September 22

1872 - Excommunication lifted in February

1873 - Travels to Rome to seek approval of the rule for her order

1875-1880 - The bishops of Brisbane and Bathurst try to run the orders in their own dioceses, against the Josephite rule; Mary withdraws her sisters from the two dioceses

1883 - Bishop of Adelaide falsely accuses Mary of drinking and embezzlement; she is expelled from the diocese

1888 - Holy See approves rule of the Institute confirming the central government of the order.

1902 - Mary suffers debilitating stroke

1909 - Dies on August 9 at the motherhouse in Sydney

1995 - Beatified by Pope John Paul II on January 19

For the Glory of God

Saint Ignatius of Loyola

1491 - 1556

The situation appeared hopeless. As the massive French army advanced toward Pamplona in northern Spain, surrender seemed the only recourse. But the captain refused to give up without a fight. On May 20, 1521, he and a handful of fellow soldiers fought valiantly for six hours before a wall in Pamplona's fortress crumbled and the attackers streamed in. When a cannon ball hit the captain—Ignatius of Loyola—and shattered his right leg, the knights surrendered and he was carried on a stretcher to his brother's castle.

The leg healed badly, slightly shorter than the other and with a bone protruding. "Because he was determined to make a way for himself in the world, he could not tolerate such ugliness and thought it marred his appearance," Ignatius wrote later in his autobiography, which he dictated in the third person. So he ordered the surgeons to remove the bump, undergoing excruciating pain for the sake of vanity.

A Greater Glory

After a near brush with death, Ignatius slowly recovered. As he lay in bed, he asked for some of the chivalrous romance novels that so fired his imagination. But his sister-in-law had only two books to give him—one on the life of Christ and the other on the lives of the saints. Soon Ignatius found himself thinking more about the great deeds of the saints than of military and romantic conquests.

One night in August 1521, Ignatius had a vision of the Blessed Mother and the child Jesus. Filled with the love of God, Ignatius said he "felt within himself a strong impulse to serve our Lord." This man, who had spent his life seeking worldly honors and fame, would now seek only to bring glory to Jesus and to bring others to him. From that point on, everything would be for "God's greater glory." Ignatius became convinced that this was the purpose for which men and women were created—to bear witness to and manifest God's divinity on earth.

Ignatius' gift to the world was his *Spiritual Exercises*, a series of meditations that grew out of his own prayer life. Wherever he went, Ignatius taught his *Exercises* to other people, hoping to move them to serve the Lord as wholeheartedly and zealously as he did. Through the Exercises Ignatius was also able to create a new army of men—the Society of Jesus—that would spread the gospel around the world, build great centers of learning, and breathe new life into the church.

A Study in Contrasts

Ignatius' life before and after his encounter with Christ is a study in contrasts. He was born in 1491 in the Basque region of northern Spain to a noble family. At the age of fifteen he was sent to a family friend—the treasurer of the king—to learn courtly manners, riding and fencing. Impulsive and arrogant, he loved wearing the brightly colored suits, flowing capes, and colored hose of the courtier, and took special pride in his flowing red hair. Eventually, Ignatius entered the military service of the Viceroy of Navarre, and it was in the Viceroy's service that he sustained the leg injury that led to his conversion.

In February 1522, Ignatius felt well enough to begin his new life serving Christ. He set off, over the protests of his brother, resolving to repent of his former life and to make a pilgrimage to Jerusalem. Ignatius gave his fancy clothes to a poor man and wore a long garment made of sackcloth. The former knight arrived in a town called Manresa, near Barcelona, where he begged for his food and let his hair grow wild to atone for the former pride he had taken in it.

Manresa would become a great school of learning for Ignatius. His long hours of prayer resulted in many mystical experiences and spiritual insights. Ignatius said at one point that God gave him an impression of the Holy Trinity as "three keys on a musical instrument," a revelation which made him sob uncontrollably.

While in Manresa, Ignatius began writing his *Spiritual Exercises*, using his own spiritual experiences as a guide. Having learned how subtle the devil was, Ignatius wrote about how to distinguish between the voice of the devil and the voice of God in prayer. He also worked out methods for discerning God's will. For instance, if someone was faced with two choices—both of them good in themselves—Ignatius'

Exercises would lead that person through prayer to determine which one was for the *greater* glory of God. All through his life, Ignatius would use these methods to pray through the decisions that faced him and his order.

Ignatius left Manresa in February 1523, determined to make his pilgrimage to Jerusalem. He sailed to Italy, sleeping outside and supporting himself by begging. He arrived in the Holy Land in September, and begged the Franciscan guardians to allow him to remain there, but they refused. With that door closed, he returned to Barcelona to "spend some time in studies in order to help souls." He enrolled in classes, a thirty-three-year-old man sitting with boys as young as twelve, memorizing Latin grammar.

After two years, Ignatius was ready to enter the university in Alcalá. By this time, he was attracting disciples and leading people through the *Spiritual Exercises*. Because the *Exercises* were so new and different, they aroused suspicion. He was even interrogated by the Inquisition and imprisoned briefly, but nothing he was teaching was contrary to the faith and he was exonerated. The same scenario was repeated in Salamanca. Eventually, he wound up at the University of Paris, where Ignatius roomed with two younger students, Peter Favre and Francis Xavier.

The First Jesuits

It was not long before Ignatius' natural warmth and understanding began to work on his roommates. Favre found that Ignatius was willing to listen to him as he sorted out what he should do with his life; he took Ignatius' spiritual advice, and was soon won over. Xavier, however, held out. Handsome, athletic and fond of a good time, he wanted no part of Ignatius' spiritual wisdom. Ignatius ignored his coolness, lending Xavier money when he could and finding students for the classes he was teaching. Finally, too, Xavier became convinced that God was calling him to a life far different than the worldly one on which he had pinned his hopes.

Four other disciples soon joined Ignatius—Diego Lainez, Alfonso Salmeron, and Nicholas Bobadilla, who were Spanish, and Simon Rodriguez, a young Portuguese student. Together, the band made the *Spiritual Exercises*. In one of the meditations in the *Exercises*, readers are faced with two choices—to stand under the banner of Christ and, like their Savior, to seek poverty, contempt, and humility, or to stand under the banner of Satan and seek riches, honor, and pride. The men chose to serve in the army of Christ.

In August 1534, on the Feast of the Assumption, they went to Montmarte in Paris to the chapel of St. Denis and made vows of poverty and chastity, along with a third vow to go to Jerusalem and convert the Muslims. If they could not get to Jerusalem, they would return to Rome and offer themselves in service to the Pope so that, as Ignatius said, "he could use them wherever he judged it would be for the greater glory of God and the good of souls." Their determination to serve the Lord out of love for him joined them together in a close bond, which would continue throughout their lives.

By 1535, Ignatius was suffering acutely from the stomach pains that had plagued him for years—the outcome of his intense fasting—and he was advised to return to his native Spain for a while to recover. He agreed to meet the other men in Italy. In the meantime, he went to his hometown of

Azpeitia. As the former proud military captain humbly preached the love of Christ, many were converted and begged him to stay. But his companions had already left Paris for Italy, so Ignatius met up with them in Venice in early 1537. Another six men had already joined them. On June 24, Ignatius and five others were ordained to the priesthood.

In the Service of Jesus

The threat of war made it impossible to travel to Jerusalem that spring, so the group decided to reevaluate the situation the following year. First, they volunteered in the hospitals, and then they broke up into small groups to preach and give the *Exercises* in different Italian cities. Ignatius went with Favre and Lainez to Rome. On the way, he saw a vision of the Father with Jesus. He heard the Father say to Jesus, "I wish you to take him as your servant." Jesus then said to Ignatius, "I wish you to be our servant." Ignatius regarded this vision as a confirmation of the name that they had chosen for their group—the Society of Jesus.

As always, while in Rome Ignatius led many—including several prominent citizens—through the *Spiritual Exercises*. By the spring of 1538, it was evident that war would again prevent the group from going to Jerusalem, so Ignatius called everyone to Rome to consider their next step.

In accord with their vow in Montmarte, the companions agreed to offer their services to the Pope. But should they add a vow of obedience to their vows of poverty and chastity and become a formal religious order? In a letter to the group, Ignatius pointed out that a religious order could multiply itself in every country on earth and continue to the end of time.

Such an order could "give those bonds of charity that unite us an eternal quality not limited by our lives."

After praying about the issue, the men agreed to the vow of obedience and unanimously elected Ignatius as the head of the order. On September 27, 1540, a papal bull establishing the Society of Jesus was signed by Pope Paul III, who lost no time in requesting several men for missionary journeys overseas. As Ignatius drew up the constitutions for the Jesuit order, he prayed over each point, seeking confirmation of the Lord's will.

Ignatius worked tirelessly as the first Father General of the Jesuits, a contemplative who almost continuously experienced the presence of God while living the most active life possible. A just and loving father to his sons, he saw many dear to his heart—like Francis Xavier—leave to reap a harvest of souls in foreign lands. Ignatius died on July 31, 1556. His spirituality has had a tremendous influence on the church that lasts to this day. Countless Christians have been led through the *Spiritual Exercises* to embrace Christ and to enter into the service of the Eternal King. In doing so, they have accomplished what Ignatius so ardently desired—they have made visible God's glory on earth.

~~≈~~ For the Glory of God ~~≈~~

St. Ignatius wrote this letter to Isabel Roser,
a noble lady and benefactor from Barcelona,
on November 10, 1532, while he was living
and studying in Paris.

You tell me of the long aliment and illness you have gone through, and of the severe stomach pains you still have. Truly, when I think of your present ill-health and pains I cannot help feeling it in my own soul, since I desire for you every imaginable well-being and prosperity which could help you for the glory and service of God our Lord. However, when I reflect that these infirmities and other temporal deprivations are often from the hand of God our Lord to help us know ourselves better and be more thoroughly rid of the love of created things and more fully aware of the brevity of this life of ours so that we will furnish ourselves for the other life which will last forever, and when I reflect that he visits with these afflictions those for whom he has great love, then I can feel no sadness or pain. For I think that through an illness a servant of God ends up with half a doctorate in how to direct and order his or her life to the glory and service of God our Lord.

Likewise, you ask my pardon if you fail to supply me with more funds, since you have many obligations to fulfill and insufficient resources. There is no reason to speak of pardon. It is about pardon for myself that I am concerned—for I fear that, if I fail to fulfill the obligations toward all my benefactors laid on me by God our Lord, his divine and righteous justice will not pardon me—all the more so in view of what I owe to you personally. In the end, if I prove unable to fulfill my responsibilities in this regard, my only hope is that, taking into account whatever merits I shall gain before the Divine Majesty (obtained through his grace, of course), the Lord himself will distribute them to those to whom I am indebted, to each person according as he has helped me in his service, and above all to you, to whom I owe a greater debt than to anyone else I know in this world. I am fully aware of this debt, and I trust in God our Lord that I will constantly deepen and increase my awareness of it. . . .

You speak of the spitefulness, intrigues, and untruths which have surrounded you on every side. I am not at all surprised at this, no matter how much worse it might be. On the day you decide, resolve, and bend every effort to work for the glory, honor, and service of God our Lord, at that moment you join battle with the world and raise your standard against it. You undertake to cast down what is lofty and embrace what is lowly, resolving to accept equally exaltation or humiliation, honor or dishonor, wealth or poverty, affection or hatred, welcome or repulse—in short, the world's glory or all its insults.

We cannot give much importance to insults in this life when they are only words. All the words in the world will never hurt a hair of our heads. Malicious, vile, and wounding words cause us pain or contentment only through our own desires in their regard. If our desire is to possess the unconditional honor and esteem of our neighbors, we will never be solidly rooted in God our Lord, or remain unscathed when we meet with affronts.

The Life of Ignatius of Loyola

1491 - Born in Loyola family castle near village of Azpeitia, in Basque region of Spain

1506 - Ignatius sent to be trained in court life in household of the king's treasurer

1521 - Injured in battle of Pamplona on May 20; experiences conversion as he recovers

1522 - In February, leaves home to begin new life; arrives in Manresa in March, where he begins writing his *Spiritual Exercises*

1523 - Leaves Manresa and travels to Jerusalem; returns to Barcelona

1524-1526 - Studies in Barcelona

1526 - Goes to University of Alcalá; interrogated by Inquisition, but cleared

1527 - Moves to Salamanca

1528 - Arrives in Paris to study at University

1534 - Makes vows of poverty and chastity with six friends on August 15 in Montmartre

1535 - Spends time in hometown of Azpeitia to recover from stomach ailment

1537 - Meets up with companions in Venice; ordained to priesthood on June 24; the group goes to Rome

1540 - Papal bull establishing the Society of Jesus issued with Ignatius as superior

1541 - Jesuits are sent to various missions around the world

1556 - Ignatius dies on July 31; the Society has one thousand members

1622 - Canonized along with fellow Jesuit Francis Xavier on March 12

God's Faithful Messenger

Saint Bridget of Sweden

1303 - 1373

Even though it was a Jubilee Year, there was little cause for joy in 1350. The Black Death gripped Europe, Rome was in ruins, and the Pope was living an opulent life in Avignon, France. Along with thousands of other pilgrims, a Swedish woman named Bridget entered the Eternal City. In a prophecy, Jesus had called her to stay in Rome until the Pope agreed to come back to St. Peter's. As it turned out, Bridget would never return to her beloved homeland.

This prophecy was one of thousands Bridget received in her lifetime—many intended for kings, emperors and pontiffs. Bridget's revelations are a testament to a God who is at the center of all that happens, both in heaven and on earth—not one who is far off and disinterested. The *Book of Revelations* recorded by this Swedish widow and mother—which would eventually fill eight volumes—shows how much God cares about political and social situations and how deeply he wants his people to come back to him. Bridget would become the Lord's mouthpiece, obedient to her prophetic vocation and faithful in the work God had given to her.

Nobility and Generosity

Bridget was the fifth of eight children, born in 1303 to noble and wealthy parents. By the age of ten, Bridget had begun experiencing visions of Mary and the crucified Christ. When she was thirteen, she married Ulf Gudmarsson, the son of a nearby nobleman. Years later, Bridget would berate herself for taking too much pride in her noble birth, but at this time in her life she acted the part of one of Sweden's great ladies, wearing the rich brocades of the day and entertaining with banquets and other festivities. Yet at the same time, she and her husband were intensely devoted to the poor. They built a hospital on their estate, and Bridget herself nursed the sick, bringing her eight children along with her to help.

The couple also undertook arduous spiritual pilgrimages. In 1343, on the way home from one such pilgrimage to the shrine of St. James of Compostela in Spain, Ulf fell seriously ill. In a vision, Bridget was consoled by St. Denis, who told her: "God will make himself known to the world through you." As a sign, the Lord allowed her husband to recover.

The trip to Spain widened Bridget's horizons. She saw up close the war raging between France and England and the problems besetting the papacy in Avignon, France. These issues would later become the subjects of some of her prophecies. At the same time, the pilgrimage seemed to be a turning point in the spiritual lives of both her and her husband.

Upon their return, they vowed to enter a religious house and dedicate their lives to the Lord. Several months later, Ulf died in a Cistercian monastery and Bridget removed her wedding ring. Her friends were shocked. "When I buried my husband," she told them, "I buried with him all earthly love." Now that he was gone, she wanted to give herself wholly to God.

The Bride of Christ

As Bridget prayed about what to do with her life, she heard the voice of the Lord: "You shall be my spouse and my instrument, and you shall hear and see spiritual things; and my Spirit shall be with you until your death." With the consent of her confessor, Bridget entered a monastery in Alvastra and began a life of intense prayer and self-denial. Women had been forbidden to enter the monastery, but Bridget managed to receive a special dispensation. Some of the monks were upset, and Bridget's own friends criticized the life she had chosen. But for the next several years, Bridget lived away from the world, until in 1346, the Lord called her to take up residence at the court of the Swedish King, Magnus II.

The thought must have been distasteful to Bridget. Before her husband had died, she had served the queen for six years as a lady-in-waiting. The king and queen were young, weak, and subject to temptations. The king was levying oppressive taxes on his people and not taking his responsibilities seriously. Bridget continually reminded him of his duties, and King Magnus made attempts at reforms that were usually short-lived. In between, he would make fun of Bridget and her visions, asking her son Birger, "What did your mother dream about us last night?"

A New Vineyard

At the time, Bridget received a startling revelation: God wanted her to start a new religious order—a "new vineyard" from which would spring fruitful branches. The revelation contained the actual rule for the order, which would be dedicated to the Blessed Virgin Mary, and called for a double monastery—one for the nuns and a separate one for monks. Bridget submitted the rule to the archbishop and other theologians, who approved it. King Magnus—once again attempting to redeem himself—deeded a royal estate near Vadstena as the site of the new monastery.

The Lord would not permit Bridget to be concerned only with the new monastery, however. She received a strong prophetic warning for Pope Clement VI, who was in Avignon, which ordered him to negotiate peace between the kings of France and England and to return to Rome. "Arise," the prophecy stated, "for your last hour is near at hand. Wipe out your past neglect by zeal at the last." Two of Bridget's friends, a bishop and a monk, went to France to deliver the prophecy and also to seek papal approval of the new order. Pope Clement did not leave France, however. Instead, he sent the bishop to negotiate with the two warring kings, which proved unsuccessful. He also withheld his approval of the new order.

In 1347, Bridget received the revelation to go to Rome. The timing probably seemed the worst possible. Not only was the Plague sweeping through Europe, but the building in Vadstena that was to become her new monastery burned to the ground. Furthermore, Bridget felt the tug of a mother's heart as she prepared to leave her children. Though most were married or in religious life, her youngest was still in school.

Still, she had given herself completely to God, that he might use her however he deemed fit. In 1349, she and several of her friends, including Father Peter, her confessor, set out for Italy. They arrived the following year.

A Light in the Darkness

Like an Old Testament prophet, Bridget lamented the state of the Eternal City: "Oh Rome, if you knew the day of your visitation, you would weep and not rejoice. Oh Rome, be converted and turn to the Lord your God." But to a city flooded in darkness, Bridget would become a light. She soon became known as the "saintly widow," who could tell whether her visitors were in sin by an intense odor and a bitter taste in her mouth. Through her prayers, many were miraculously healed. This woman, who had been one of the richest in Sweden, now lived in complete dependence on God. Once she asked the Virgin Mary if she should do manual work to support herself and her friends. Mary told her to continue praying and writing. If she had nothing left to eat, she should beg.

In that same Jubilee year, Bridget's daughter Katherine came to visit her. Although Katherine was married, Bridget appeared to know in advance that her husband would soon die and that Katherine was to stay in Rome as Bridget's helper. As Katherine prepared to leave Rome, Bridget asked her to stay, and she agreed. Soon afterwards, Katherine learned that her husband had indeed died in Sweden.

For seventeen years, Bridget continued to pray, wait on the Lord, record her prophecies, and urge the popes to return to Rome. Finally, in 1367, Pope Urban V did return. Bridget immediately sent him a letter revealing her vision of the church as a decayed and filthy building that must be repaired through humility, simplicity, and almsgiving. She also asked once more that her religious order be approved.

While Bridget awaited the Pope's answer, the Lord told her to go on a pilgrimage to Amalfi, Italy, to venerate the relics of St. Andrew. For once Bridget protested: "Oh, Lord, time is slipping away. Old age and infirmity are coming on me, and money is melting!" However, the Lord promised to give her strength and grace. She relented and traveled to and from Amalfi unharmed in any way.

When she returned to Rome, Bridget learned that Pope Urban was planning to go back to France. She pleaded with him to remain and prophesied that he would die shortly after arriving in France. But Urban left, and Bridget's prophecy was fulfilled. The Pope died in December 1370, shortly after approving the rule for Bridget's order.

While the building of the monastery at Vadstena resumed, Bridget made no plans to return to her homeland. She felt she could not leave Rome until she fulfilled the second part of her mission: To see the new Pope, Gregory XI, return to the Holy See. However, the Lord sent her away again—this time on a pilgrimage to Jerusalem. On the way, her group of twelve—which included Bridget's two sons—stopped in Naples to visit Queen Joanna. Charles, Bridget's "son of tears," was immediately attracted to the Queen, although both were married. Bridget cried and prayed that her son might die rather than lose his soul. When he suddenly became ill and died, Bridget had a vision that Mary had taken his soul under protection.

A Witness to Christ's Birth and Death

A special revelation was to greet Bridget in the Holy Land. At the site of Jesus' crucifixion, she witnessed Christ's death as if it were taking place before her. The powerful vision was recorded in her *Book of Revelations* and greatly influenced religious art for centuries. The famous *Piéta*, of Mary holding her dead Son in her arms, is one of the scenes Bridget described in her revelations. In a similar way, when she arrived in Bethlehem, she witnessed Mary and the baby Jesus on that first Christmas night.

Bridget returned to Rome an old and failing woman. For the first time in her life, a dark night engulfed her and she wondered how the work that God had given her to do would ever be accomplished. However, Jesus assured her that she would be counted as a nun of Vadstena, if not literally, then at least spiritually. On July 23, 1373, she died, three years before another great saint, Catherine of Siena, would welcome Pope Gregory on his return to Rome. Bridget's body was taken to Vadstena, where her Order of the Most Holy Savior, known as the Bridgettines, flourished. Bridget would be counted first among them.

God's Faithful Messenger

When St. Bridget traveled to the Holy Land
at the end of her life, she was privileged
to experience a revelation of the crucifixion,
witnessing it as if it were taking place
before her. The vision is recorded in the
Seventh Book of Revelations of St. Bridget.

His fine and lovely eyes appeared half dead; his
mouth was open and bloody; his face was pale and
sunken, all livid and stained with blood; and his
whole body was as if black and blue and pale and very weak
from the constant downward flow of blood. Indeed, his skin
and the virginal flesh of his most holy body were so delicate
and tender that, after the infliction of a slight blow, a black
and blue mark appeared on the surface. At times, however,
he tried to make stretching motions on the cross because of
the exceeding bitterness of the intent and most acute pain
that he felt. For at times the pain from his pierced limbs and
veins ascended to his heart and battered him cruelly with an
intense martyrdom; and thus his death was prolonged and
delayed amidst grave torment and great bitterness.

Then, therefore, in distress from the exceeding anguish
of his pain and already near to death, Jesus cried to the Father
in a loud and tearful voice, saying: "O Father, why have you
forsaken me?" He then had pale lips, a bloody tongue, and a
sunken abdomen that adhered to his back as if he had no vis-
cera within. A second time also, he cried out again in the
greatest of pain and anxiety: "O Father, into you hands I com-
mend my spirit." Then his head, raising itself a little, imme-

diately bowed; and thus he sent forth his spirit. When his Mother then saw these things, she trembled at that immense bitterness and would have fallen onto the earth if she had not been supported by the other women. Then, in that hour, his hands retracted slightly from the place of the nail holes because of the exceeding weight of his body; and thus his body was as if supported by the nails with which his feet had been crucified. Moreover, his fingers and hands and arms were not more extended than before; his shoulder blades, in fact, and his back were as if pressed tightly to the cross.

Then at last the people standing around cried out in mockery against his Mother, saying many things. For some said: "Mary, now your Son is dead," but others said other mocking words. And while the crowds were thus standing about, one man came running with the greatest of fury and fixed a lance in his right side with such violence and force that the lance would have passed almost through the other side of the body. Thus, when the lance was extracted from the body, at once a stream, as it were, of blood spurted out of that wound in abundance; in fact, the iron blade of the lance and a part of the shaft came out of the body red and stained with the blood. Seeing these things, his Mother so violently trembled with bitter sighing that it was quite discernible in her face and bearing that her soul was then being penetrated by the sharp sword of sorrow.

When all these things had been accomplished and when the large crowds were receding, certain of the Lord's friends took him down. Then, with pity, his Mother received him into her most holy arms; and sitting, she laid him on her knee, all torn as he was and wounded and black and blue. With tears, she and John and those others, the weeping women, washed him. And then, with her linen cloth, his most mournful Mother wiped his whole body and its wounds. And she closed his eyes and kissed them; and she wrapped him in a clean cloth of fine linen. And thus they escorted him with lamentation and very great sorrow and placed him in the sepulchre.

The Life of Bridget of Sweden

1303 - Born on June 14, the fifth child of a wealthy noble family

1313 - Experiences first supernatural visions

1316 - Marries Ulf Gudmarsson, the son of a nearby nobleman, at the age of thirteen

1335 - Becomes chief lady-in-waiting for the Swedish queen

1343 - Ulf and Bridget make pilgrimage to Spain and vow to enter religious life after returning to Sweden

1344 - Ulf dies in monastery at Alvastra; Bridget begins life of prayer and penance in monastery

1346 - Takes up residence at the court of the Swedish King, Magnus II; receives revelation to start new religious order

1347 - Receives revelation to go to Rome; monastery intended for Bridget's order burns

1350 - Arrives in Rome with friends and confessor; Bridget's daughter, Katherine, comes to visit and stays

1367 - Pope Urban V temporarily returns to Rome

1370 - Rule for Bridget's order approved by Pope Urban

1371 - Makes pilgrimage to Holy Land, where she witnesses Christ's birth and death in special revelations

1373 - Dies on July 23 in Rome; her body is taken to the Swedish monastery of her religious order

1391 - Bridget is canonized by Pope Boniface IX

A Passion for Souls

Saint Anthony Mary Claret

1807 - 1870

Anthony Claret possessed all the gifts to become a world-renowned designer. Born in 1807 in the small town of Sallent in Catalonia, Spain, Anthony was the son of a weaver and entered the family business as a teenager. He excelled beyond anyone's expectations. At seventeen, he accepted an apprenticeship in Barcelona, where he continued to study the fabric industry. New designs, both of fabrics and of the machines that produced them, consumed him. Nothing could deter this single-minded young man from his goal. "There were more machines in my head than saints on the altar," he would later confess.

Claret's growing obsession began to make him uneasy, however. Like his parents, he had always been devout. Impressed by thoughts of eternity as a young child, he would lie awake at night repeating the words *para siempre*—"forever." But now his relationship with the Lord was being crowded out by the distractions of his profession. One day in 1828, as he was walking along the beach, a huge wave knocked him off his feet and carried him out to sea, beyond the reach of his friends. Unable to swim, he cried out to the Virgin Mary and found himself immediately on shore. The miracle served as a wake-up call, and he decided to abandon his profession and become a priest.

The switch of vocations, however, didn't change Claret's single-minded personality. Now, instead of machines and fabrics, he became consumed with saving souls. The word "forever" was deeply etched on his soul. No one was beyond hope. Everyone could live with Jesus forever. From remote villages to royal courts, and across the ocean, Anthony Claret would preach this message. Through his printed words and the missionary order he founded, millions more would hear the Good News of Jesus Christ.

The Missionary Call

Claret was ordained in 1835 and sent to his hometown of Sallent to become the parish priest there. Even in priestly garb, his physical presence was unassuming. Just over five feet tall, he possessed irregular features, a large round head and dark brown eyes. Nevertheless, the villagers were overjoyed at welcoming home their twenty-seven-year-old native son. But he would not stay for long. Over the next few years, his desire to become a missionary and preach to people who had never heard the gospel only intensified. In 1839, over the protests of his parishioners, Claret obtained permission from his bishop to go to Rome and offer himself to the church as a missionary.

In Rome, Claret was introduced to a Jesuit priest who invited him to become a missionary with his order. Claret was overjoyed and made the traditional thirty-day *Spiritual Exercises* of St. Ignatius Loyola. However, after several happy months as a novice, God made it clear that Anthony was not to remain in Rome. He was suddenly attacked by a severe pain in his leg, which his superiors took as a sign that he should return to Spain. In 1840, Claret sailed back to Catalonia, where he was appointed regent of Viladrau, a remote mountain town. His leg pain disappeared as mysteriously as it had come.

In Viladrau, Claret encountered a populace plunged in despair, its sick and dying unattended. The village had been sacked by opposing political factions in a bloody civil war, and all of its physicians had fled. "What else could I do," he wrote, "but become a doctor of corporal as well as spiritual ailments, especially since I possessed a certain knowledge of medicine which I had studied from books?" Using simple herbs and oils, the priest-turned-physician was soon producing numerous cures.

Healing the Sick and Captivating Hearts

As word of Claret's healing powers spread, throngs of people sought him out. However, because he was so busy with preaching and hearing confessions, "I found it inconvenient to prescribe physical remedies." Instead, he simply made the sign of the cross over them and repeated the words from Scripture, "They will lay their hands on the sick, and they will recover" (Mark 16:18). And recover they did—by the scores. Claret recognized that God was healing the people because they had repented of their sins. "Our Lord captivated their hearts by these corporal cures," Claret marveled.

Not only did people throng to Claret; his superiors instructed him to travel to small towns all over Catalonia giving missions and retreats. Walking along the mountainous trails of the Pyrenees through snowstorms and intense heat, Claret determined that he would reach his flock whatever the personal cost. Calling sinners "our dear brothers," he yearned for their return to the Lord and he devoted his life to bringing them back. He rarely slept more than two hours each night. When he wasn't preaching, he was writing down his sermons and distributing them in little tracts which were enthusiastically received.

Claret was always careful to avoid siding with any political faction. However, with anti-clericalism on the rise in Spain, the bishop feared Claret—now very popular for his healings and his preaching—might be in danger. In 1848, Claret was sent to safety in the Canary Islands, where his preaching and healing once again produced great crowds. Still, busy as he was, Claret continued writing religious books at night.

When he returned to Catalonia in 1849, Claret launched two projects that would expand his missionary reach. His writing had been so successful that he turned over the work to a commercial printing house, which would continue to distribute his books. He also received approval to found a new congregation, the Missionary Sons of the Immaculate Heart of Mary. The first five candidates made the *Spiritual Exercises*, and Claret was unanimously elected their superior.

Archbishop and Reformer

While immersed in establishing his order, Claret's life took an unexpected turn: He was asked to become Archbishop of Santiago in Cuba. At first, he was stunned. Why would the Lord want him to leave the work he was doing while it was still in its infancy? "On the one hand," he wrote, "I did not see how I could possibly accept; and on the other, I wanted to be obedient." Although he had never desired to be anything more than a simple priest, Claret decided that this was indeed God's will.

He arrived in Cuba in 1851 to find the spiritual welfare of the people in even worse shape than he had imagined. There were only a few priests—many of whom were unfit—and many of the couples were not legitimately married. In addition, those interested in independence were far from excited to greet a Spanish cleric who they thought represented oppressive rule.

Characteristically, Claret plunged into action. He visited remote areas where most people had never seen a bishop. He required all the priests to take the *Spiritual Exercises*. He spoke out fearlessly against slavery—an outlawed but still common practice in Cuba—and racial discrimination in general. He also distributed alms every Sunday and established a parish savings bank system to encourage the acquisition of small independent farms. Moved by the thousands of orphans that lived on the streets, Claret built a large school and farm for them. He even wrote a book about good agricultural practices. There seemed to be no end to the challenges Claret would take on out of concern for his people.

Not surprisingly, Claret's shake-up of the status quo won him many enemies. After several attempts on his life, on February 1, 1856, he was attacked by a man wielding a knife. The man missed his throat, but slashed his face, disfiguring him from his chin to his cheekbone. Claret bled profusely, but was not in mortal danger. "I cannot describe the . . . happiness my soul knew in the attainment of what I had so long desired: to shed my blood for the love of Jesus and Mary."

Confessor to the Queen

In 1857, Claret was recalled to Spain—for another wholly unexpected assignment. Queen Isabel wanted him to come to Madrid to act as her personal confessor. Claret was again stunned. "In the entire episcopate, there is no one less suited to this office, none with less affinity to the palace," he wrote to a friend. Still, the papal representative in Spain urged him to accept the position, and he agreed only on condition that he would not reside at the palace. The appointment would leave him time to preach, study, and continue writing. Besides, while the king and queen were away, he could travel from city to city preaching the gospel.

Claret believed that his past experiences had infused into him a love of persecution, and that was confirmed when, in early 1859, he received a prophecy that he would become "like the earth . . . which is trampled upon, yet doesn't speak." In the mid-1860s, revolutionaries anxious to unseat the monarchy began to spread vicious rumors about the queen's confessor. They said it was really he who ruled the country, and accused him of a variety of outrageous offenses, including sexual impropriety and theft. In imitation of Jesus, Claret refused to defend himself. Finally, in 1868, a successful uprising forced the royal family—and Claret—into exile. His congregation was also banished to the French Pyrenees.

The exile brought with it freedom. Claret no longer felt obligated to act as confessor to the queen, who was expected to abdicate. He went instead to Rome to prepare for the First

Vatican Council where, in 1870, he successfully persuaded his fellow bishops to define the doctrine of papal infallibility. When the Council closed, one of the priests from his order went to Rome to bring him back to Spain. Their hope was that what little remained of his own life—spent so lavishly on the gospel—would now be spent within his religious family.

But it was not meant to be. When the Spanish revolutionaries discovered his whereabouts, they set out to capture him. Fortunately, before Claret could be seized, the priests hid him in a remote Cistercian monastery in France. He died several months later, on October 24, 1870—cut off from the country where he had preached so ardently and from the brothers in the community he had founded. However, his work on earth was complete. His order, which became known as the Claretians, multiplied, satisfying his undying passion to bring souls to the Lord.

A Passion for Souls

In his autobiography, written towards the end of his life, St. Anthony Claret explained why he was so determined to preach the gospel.

Whenever I went to a town, I did so without any worldly goal in mind; my only aim was to glorify God and save souls. I was often forced to remind people of this because I knew that it was the most convincing argument for good and bad alike. I would tell them:

You know that men nearly always do whatever it is they do for one or another of the follow reasons: (1) for gain or money, (2) for pleasure, (3) for fame. I have not come to preach a mission in this town for any of these three reasons. Not for money, because I don't want a penny from anyone and I won't take one. Not for pleasure, for what pleasure could I get out of wearing myself out from early in the morning until night? . . . Maybe I do it for fame? Hardly. You must be well aware of the calumnies I'm exposed to. One person may praise me, but another makes all sorts of charges against me. . . .

No, I repeat, I have no mere earthly aim but a far nobler one. My aim is to make God better known, loved, and served by everyone. If only I had all human hearts, with which to love God! My God, people do not know you! If they did, you would be loved far more than you are. If people only knew your wisdom, power, goodness, beauty, and all your divine attributes, they would all have become seraphim consumed with the fire of your divine love. This is my aim: to make God known, so that He may be loved and served by all. . . .

Tell me, if you had a very dear brother who was so sick that he was delirious and in his fever insulted you and said every foul thing in the world to you, would you abandon him? I'm sure you wouldn't. You'd feel all the more sorry for him and do everything you could for his recovery. Well, that's the way I feel about sinners. The poor creatures are just delirious. That makes them all the more deserving of compassion. I can't abandon them. I have to work for their salvation and pray to God for them, saying with Jesus Christ, "Father, forgive them, for they don't know what they're doing or saying.". . .

To give you an idea of how I feel, I'll draw a comparison. If a loving mother saw her child in danger of falling from a high window or into an open fireplace, wouldn't she run and shout, "Look out, baby, you're going to fall!" Wouldn't she run up behind the child and take hold of him, and pull him back if she could? My brothers and sisters, you should know that grace is stronger and braver than nature. Well then, if the natural love a mother feels for her child can make her run to him, shout at him, take hold of him, and pull him back from the brink of ruin, that is just what grace does in me. . . .

Another force that drives me to preach and hear confessions is my desire to make my neighbor happy. If there is so much joy in healing the sick, freeing the prisoner, consoling the afflicted, and cheering the sad, then there is far greater joy in bringing one's neighbor to the glory of heaven. It means saving him from every evil and bringing him to the enjoyment of every good— and for all eternity. Mortals cannot understand this just now, but when they are in glory they will know the great good that was offered them and that they will have, happily, attained. Then they will sing the everlasting mercies of the Lord and bless those who have been merciful to them.

The Life of Anthony Mary Claret

1807 - Born on December 24 in Sallent in Catalonia, Spain

1825 - Accepts apprenticeship in weaving and fabric design in Barcelona

1828 - Miraculously rescued from ocean; decides to become priest

1835 - Ordained on June 13 and sent to hometown parish

1839 - Obtains permission to go to Rome to become missionary

1840 - Returns to Spain because of leg ailment; becomes regent of Viladrau; preaching and healing ministry begins

1848 - Sent to safety in Canary Islands

1849 - Returns to Catalonia and begins larger publishing endeavor; receives approval for new congregation

1851 - Arrives in Cuba as Archbishop of Santiago

1856 - Attempt on his life on February 1

1857 - Recalled to Spain to become personal confessor to Queen Isabel

1868 - Uprising forces Claret and his congregation into exile

1870 - Participates in First Vatican Council; dies on October 24 in remote Cistercian monastery in France

1950 - Canonized by Pope Pius XII on May 7

I Have Called You by Name

Making Disciples of All Nations

Saints Cyril and Methodius

827 - 869 • 815 - 885

Our God is a God of surprises who often works in unexpected ways to bring his saving truth to his people. To carry out his plans, he needs disciples who are courageous, creative, and filled with faith. In the ninth century, God chose two such men—Cyril and Methodius—to bring the Good News of Jesus Christ to the Slavonic people in their own language. Although they would have preferred to stay in their monastery, these men followed God's call with a burning zeal. Their mission would have a profound impact on the Slavic nations, both culturally and spiritually, and they would eventually become known as the Apostles to the Slavs.

Cyril and Methodius were brothers and monks. Because Slavs had taken up residence outside their city of Thessalonica many years before, they were familiar with Slavonic. They were the perfect choice for a missionary outreach to Moravia, a formerly pagan nation outside the Holy Roman and Byzantine Empires that had recently embraced Christianity.

Called Back into the World

Cyril was the youngest of seven children. Born in 827, he was baptized Constantine. Methodius was born around 815. Their parents were wealthy Christians of the noble class, and both brothers were well educated. At the age of sixteen, Cyril began studies in philosophy at the imperial school in Constantinople, and eventually became a renowned professor of philosophy. Methodius worked as a civil administrator.

Despite their worldly successes, both men felt drawn to religious life. Methodius entered a monastery on Mount Olympus, where he was made abbot. Cyril was ordained a priest and, in 855, he joined his brother as a monk. There, on Olympus, they pursued a life of prayer and contemplation.

Yet political concerns would soon sweep the two brothers back into the world they had abandoned. In 860, Emperor Michael II, head of the Byzantine empire, sent a delegation to the Khazar Empire in the Ukraine. The mission was diplomatic—the emperor wanted to make sure the Khazars would come to his aid in case the Byzantine Empire was attacked from the north. Cyril and Methodius were asked to join the delegation.

The Search for Relics

Cyril knew the group would be passing through the Crimea, where St. Clement I—the third successor of St. Peter—was said to be buried on a small island near the city of Cherson. He was determined to find the grave. When they arrived in Cherson, Cyril convinced the archbishop to assemble a search party. They set out early on January 30, 861, singing praises to God and invoking the intercession of St. Clement.

According to tradition, St. Clement was cast into the sea with an anchor tied to him while in exile in Crimea in the first century. When bones were excavated near the ruins of an old church—along with an anchor—the search party believed they had discovered the saint's remains and returned to the city rejoicing.

Cyril and Methodius returned home from the Ukraine weary and anxiously looking forward to resuming their monastic life. However, only a few months later, Prince Rastislav of Moravia petitioned the emperor to send a bishop and teacher to his nation, located in the present-day Czech Republic.

Developing a Written Language

When asked about the mission, Cyril hesitated. The Slavs did not have a written language. How could he possibly disseminate the gospel without one? Furthermore, no one had ever been able to produce a Slavonic alphabet. When Cyril pointed this out to the emperor, he replied, "If you are willing, you can do it, with the help of God, who gives to all who ask with confidence and opens to those who knock."

Over the next several months, Cyril developed a Slavonic script and began translating the gospels. When the delegation was ready to depart, the missionaries carried a precious gift—the newly translated books. A message to Prince Rastislav from the emperor said, "God has accomplished in our time what until now has never been done: He has made known a system of letters for your language that you also may become a great nation, whose people will glorify God in their own tongue."

Although Prince Rastislav truly wanted Christian missionaries, his request to the Byzantine emperor was not entirely spiritual. His country had recently become independent of Germany, and he was looking for an ally in the East to help ward off future attacks. To ensure his independence, he sought a separate church hierarchy—not one under the German bishops. Undeterred by the politics of the situation, the Lord would use even these motives to bring his word to his people.

Cyril and Methodius spent nearly four years in Moravia. They used the Slavonic language in their preaching and in the Masses they celebrated. Although it was the custom in the East to use the native language in the liturgy, it was virtually unheard of in the Western tradition. So, while their missionary efforts met with immediate success, the German priests in the country were incensed. They had first evangelized the area—although with marginal results—and questioned the right of the Greek missionaries to be in Moravia in the first place.

The Journey to Rome

Whether they were summoned to Rome or decided to go on their own, the brothers set out in 867 to meet with the Pope. He would have to settle the question of the Slavonic liturgy. They brought with them some disciples, all Slavs, who hoped to be ordained by the Pope.

Along the way, in Venice, church officials questioned Cyril and Methodius: "Why this production of books for the Slavs, and why this use of them in the liturgy? Such a thing has never been done before." They insisted that only three languages—Hebrew, Greek, and Latin—were appropriate for liturgical worship. Cyril was convinced that his missionary success was due largely to his use of the native language, and cited the words of St. Paul to the Philippians: "Every tongue shall confess that Jesus Christ is Lord" (2:11).

The group arrived triumphantly in Rome, bringing with them the relics of St. Clement. Pope Hadrian II seemed to recognize that God was working in a new way, and that Cyril and Methodius were pioneers in that work through the Slavonic liturgy. He blessed the Slavonic liturgical books and placed them on the altar. The Slavonic disciples were ordained, and the Pope reestablished an ancient See covering Moravia and nearby Pannonia (modern-day Hungary) that would be independent from the German hierarchy.

"A Servant . . . of God Almighty"

Before they could return to Moravia, however, Cyril fell ill. Sensing that he was near death, he donned monastic robes once more. "From now on," he said, "I am no longer a servant of the emperor or of anyone else, but only of God Almighty." Although he had always been called by his baptismal name of Constantine, he chose his new name in honor of St. Cyril of Alexandria. On February 14, 869, a mere fifty days after accepting the monastic habit, Cyril died at the age of forty-two. He was buried in the Church of St. Clement in Rome, alongside the relics he had discovered.

Before his death, Cyril made his brother promise that he would complete the work that they had started together, rather than retire to a monastery. Methodius was consecrated Archbishop of the new See, and soon left for Pannonia, where he was enthusiastically greeted by Prince Kocel.

The German bishops were far from happy with the situation, however. They accused Methodius of trespassing on their territory. "If I believed it was yours," said Methodius, "I would depart, but it rightfully belongs to St. Peter." While being questioned by the bishops, someone remarked how much he was perspiring. He replied, "I have been sparring with slow-witted men."

Imprisoned by a Bishop

Without permitting any appeals to Rome, the German bishops imprisoned Methodius for two and one-half years. When the Pope, newly elected John VIII, found out that Methodius was in prison, he demanded his release. "What kind of bishop is he who thus injures a brother-bishop?" he asked.

Out of prison, Methodius immediately set to work. These were the most productive years of his ministry. He reopened the seminary, assigned priests to the local towns, baptized new believers, and traveled to visit his flock in every part of the territory.

Despite these successes, more trials awaited Methodius. In 879, a German priest went to Rome to lodge a complaint, charging Methodius with teaching heresies and with using Slavonic in the liturgy. Methodius traveled to Rome, where he successfully defended himself against the charges. The Pope once again sanctioned the Slavonic liturgy, as long as the Scriptures were read first in Latin.

Unfortunately, a German priest named Wiching—who fiercely opposed Methodius—was appointed one of his bishops. Wiching was in Rome at the same time as Methodius, but rushed home before him to spread false rumors that the Pope had condemned and deposed the archbishop. He even forged a papal bull that named him as the rightful archbishop. It took several letters back and forth from Rome to set the record straight.

During his last few years, Methodius completed the translations from Greek into Slavonic of all of the books of the Old Testament. Beloved and surrounded by the Slovak people, he died on March 6, 885.

Apostles to the Slavs

The controversy over the Slavonic liturgy and ecclesiastic jurisdiction continued after his death. Disciples of Methodius were eventually expelled from Moravia but became missionaries in surrounding Slavic countries. In 907, the Great Moravian Empire collapsed under the attack of pagan Hungarians. Yet, the legacy of Saints Cyril and Methodius could not be destroyed. They had placed their lives before God, to use as he willed. He used them to bring not only a written language to the Slavs but the saving knowledge of Jesus Christ.

Pope John Paul II praised the evangelistic efforts of Sts. Cyril and Methodius in a 1985 encyclical entitled *Slavorum Apostoli*, commemorating eleven centuries since the death of St. Methodius in 885.

E ven though Slav Christians, more than others, tend to think of the holy Brothers as "Slavs at heart," the latter nevertheless remain men of Hellenic culture and Byzantine training. In other words, men who fully belonged to the civil and ecclesiastical tradition of the Christian East.

Already in their time certain differences between Constantinople and Rome had begun to appear as pretexts for disunity, even though the deplorable split between the two parts of the same Christian world was still in the distant future. The evangelizers and teachers of the Slavs set out for Greater Moravia imbued with all the wealth of tradition and religious experience which marked Eastern Christianity and which was particularly evident in theological teaching and in the celebration of the Sacred Liturgy.

The sacred rites in all the Churches within the borders of the Byzantine Empire had long been celebrated in Greek. However, the traditions of many national Churches of the East, such as the Georgian and Syriac, which used the language of the people in their liturgies, were well known to the advanced cultural milieu of Constantinople. They were especially well known to Constantine the Philosopher

[Cyril], as a result of his studies and of his many contacts with Christians belonging to those Churches, both in the capital and in the course of his journeys.

Both the Brothers were aware of the antiquity and legitimacy of these traditions, and were therefore not afraid to use the Slavonic language in the liturgy and to make it into an effective instrument for bringing the divine truths to those who spoke it. This they did without any spirit of superiority or domination, but out of love of justice and with a clear apostolic zeal for peoples then developing. . . .

At this point it is an unusual and admirable thing that the holy Brothers, working in such complex and precarious situations, did not seek to impose on the peoples assigned to their preaching either the undeniable superiority of the Greek language and Byzantine culture, or the customs and way of life of the more advanced society in which they had grown up and which necessarily remained familiar and dear to them. Inspired by the ideal of uniting in Christ the new believers, they adapted to the Slavonic language the rich and refined texts of the Byzantine liturgy and likewise adapted to the mentality and customs of the new peoples the subtle and complex elaborations of Greco-Roman law. In following this program of harmony and peace, Cyril and Methodius were ever respectful of the obligations of their mission. . . . Thus, though subjects of the Eastern Empire and believers subject to the Patriarchate of Constantinople, they considered it their duty to give an account of their missionary work to the Roman Pontiff. They likewise submitted to his judgment, in order to obtain his approval, the doctrine which they professed and taught, the liturgical books which they had written in the Slavonic language, and the methods which they were using in evangelizing those peoples.

Having undertaken their mission under orders from Constantinople, they then in a sense sought to have it confirmed by approaching the Apostolic See of Rome, the visible center of the Church's unity. Thus they established the Church with an awareness of her universality as one, holy, catholic and apostolic. This is clearly and explicitly seen in their whole way of acting. It can be said that Jesus' priestly prayer—*ut unum sint* (John 17:21)—is their missionary motto in accordance with the Psalmist's words: "Praise the Lord, all nations! Extol him, all peoples" (117:1). For us today their apostolate also possesses the eloquence of an ecumenical appeal: it is an invitation to restore, in the peace of reconciliation, the unity that was gravely damaged after the time of Cyril and Methodius, and, first and foremost, the unity between East and West.

The Lives of Cyril and Methodius

c. 815 - Methodius born in Thessalonica to wealthy Christian parents

827 - Cyril, the youngest of seven children and brother to Methodius, is born

843 - Cyril begins studies in philosophy in Constantinople

1840 - Methodius retires from civil government to become monk in monastery on Mount Olympus

850 - Cyril assumes chair in philosophy at imperial school

855 - Cyril ordained a priest; joins Methodius on Mount Olympus

860 - Cyril and Methodius join delegation to Khazar Empire in the Ukraine

861 - Remains of St. Clement discovered

862 - Return from Khazar mission; Cyril and Methodius chosen for delegation to Moravia

863 - Delegation arrives in Moravia with translations of gospels in Slavonic; Cyril and Methodius begin missionary work among Slavs

867 - Brothers set out for Rome to meet with Pope Hadrian II, who blesses Slavonic liturgical books

869 - Cyril dies in Rome on February 14, fifty days after donning monastic habit; Methodius consecrated archbishop of newly created See independent of German hierarchy

870 - German bishops imprison Methodius

873 - Methodius released through intervention of Pope John VIII and reinstated in Moravia

879 - German priest lodges complaint against Methodius

880 - Methodius goes to Rome to defend himself against charges of heresy and using the Slavonic liturgy; Pope publishes bull vindicating him

881 - German bishop Wiching forges papal bull naming himself as the rightful archbishop; Pope John sets records straight

885 - Methodius dies on March 6

A Magnet for Christ

Saint Francis de Sales

1567 - 1622

If there had been a bestseller book list in 1609, *Introduction to the Devout Life* would have been at the top. Perhaps it was unusual even in the seventeenth century for a spiritual book to become so popular, but there was a reason that this one—written by the well-loved Bishop of Geneva, Francis de Sales—hit a chord with so many. Its premise was revolutionary: Even if you were not in a religious order, you could lead a life pleasing to God. The laborer, the shopkeeper, the wife and mother—all could discover God's immense love for them.

Francis attracted people to the Lord by his writing, but he was even more of a magnet for Christ in person. In fact, many said he personified Christ. Gentle, gracious, good-natured, and wise, he was not afraid to show his love to others, even though his office as bishop could have caused him to distance himself from his flock. A master spiritual director, he possessed a keen understanding of human nature that enabled him to give practical, realistic advice to guide people in their journey to God.

Francis de Sales was born on August 21, 1567, in the Alpine region of Savoy, now part of eastern France but then an independent duchy. He was the oldest child of a retired soldier who pinned great hopes on a stellar law career for his son. At the age of fourteen, Francis went to Paris to study with the Jesuits, where his devotion to God grew. Even during a brief spiritual crisis when he was nineteen and feared he would never get to heaven, he was able to pray, "Whatever happens, Lord, may I at least love you in this life if I cannot love you in eternity."

Although Francis completed his law studies in Padua, Italy, he knew he wanted to become a priest. To ameliorate his father's disappointment, his cousin obtained a position of rank for him in the church. Francis was ordained on December 18, 1593, and became provost of the diocese.

Love Will Shake the Walls

Full of zeal, the young provost volunteered for a harrowing missionary trip to Chablais, to the south of Lake Geneva. The Swiss had invaded the area some sixty years earlier, persecuting Catholics and forcing them to become Calvinists. In September 1594, de Sales and his cousin Louis went to Chablais on foot, hoping to reconvert the region's sixty thousand inhabitants to Catholicism. Yet de Sales was determined to accomplish this without the Duke's military assistance: "Love will shake the walls of Geneva. By love we must invade it; by love we must conquer it."

The first years were rough and discouraging. Only about one hundred people had remained Catholic, and just a few of them were courageous enough to venture out publicly to attend a Mass. Consequently, de Sales often preached to the walls. Undaunted, he trudged door to door in the frigid Alpine winter, crossing a dangerous ice-covered bridge on his hands and knees each morning. When he saw that this too was bearing little fruit, he finally decided to write doctrinal pamphlets which he could distribute by hand and leave in public places. Slowly, these began to make an impact, and Francis's writing ministry was born.

By Christmas 1596, Francis felt it was safe enough to say a public Mass in Thonon, the chief city of Chablais. The next year, he distributed ashes on Ash Wednesday, which so angered some of his opponents that he had to flee for his life from the church. Nevertheless, he led a large procession with the Blessed Sacrament that fall, with thousands of people in attendance. At a similar but larger procession the following year, many Protestants asked to be received into the Catholic Church. De Sales was becoming known as the "Apostle of Chablais."

Around this time, Francis's bishop, Claude de Granier, failing in health, was anxious to name de Sales as his successor. Francis saw the post as too heavy a burden and asked to be spared. But a fellow priest encouraged him to offer a Mass to the Holy Spirit to find what God wanted him to do. Francis agreed. After kneeling on the altar in prayer and ecstasy, he felt ready to accept the post.

Preaching Love and Mercy

In 1602, de Sales traveled to Paris on diplomatic/church business. With his simple, heart-to-heart approach to preaching—and with his emphasis on the mercy and love of God—

his popularity in the city grew. He was soon accepting numerous invitations to preach, even from the royal court. King Henry IV was especially impressed and offered him the opportunity for a larger, more important diocese. But de Sales replied, "I have married a poor wife, and I cannot desert her for a richer one."

On the way back from Paris, de Sales learned of Bishop de Granier's death. He would now become Bishop of Geneva. During his Mass of Consecration, in December 1602, Francis had a vision of the Trinity working powerfully within him. It was a defining moment for him, as he later explained: God "took me away from myself, to make me his own, and to give me in turn to the people."

The grace of this experience was evident in the way in which de Sales threw himself into his duties, even as he continued to write books and numerous letters of spiritual direction. One of his favorite activities was to personally teach Sunday catechism classes, especially to the children. Even though Francis' diocese spanned remote mountain villages, he made it a point to visit each parish, reaching the peasants on horseback in all kinds of weather and conversing with them in their own dialect. "It is one of God's little miracles," he once wrote. "Every day I am so tired that I cannot move body or spirit; but in the morning I am brighter than ever."

Despite his busy schedule, in 1604 Francis accepted an invitation to preach the Lenten sermons in nearby Dijon. Before he left, he had a vision of a young widow, and knew that God wanted him to found a religious order with the woman, although he did not know who she was. The newly appointed bishop of Dijon was André de Frémyot, whose sister, Jeanne de Chantal, had been widowed for several years. Two years earlier, she too had received a vision—of an unknown bishop—and heard a voice saying, "Here is the guide, beloved of God and men, in whose hands you must put your conscience." When the two saw each other in the church in Dijon, there was a spark of recognition. The meeting was to begin one of the most famous spiritual friendships of all time.

A Union of Hearts

The young widow was desolate and sought Francis' advice and direction. He agreed, and in one of his first letters to her, Francis wrote out spiritual exercises—with one word of caution: "Everything must be done through love, nothing through force. Obedience must be loved rather than disobedience feared." Although Jeanne desired formal religious life, Francis urged patience and reminded her that "nothing so impedes our progress in perfection as to be sighing after another way of life."

Under Francis' direction, Jeanne's spiritual life blossomed, and their friendship grew. "My daughter," Francis wrote in one letter, "God has given me a special light and shown me that the union of our hearts is his work. . . . I desire to look upon it as something sacred."

In 1607, Francis told Jeanne of his plans to found a new religious congregation, with her as its superior. He wanted to create a community that would not exclude women whose health might not permit them to endure the rigorous lifestyles of some stricter orders. Jeanne's youngest child was only six years old, so they assumed that nothing could be done for a long time. Yet in only three years, enough changes had taken place in Jeanne's life to make it possible to launch the congregation, with her young daughter living with her. And so, in 1610, the Institute of the Visitation was begun with three women living in a small house in Annecy.

The Devout Life

In the meantime, de Sales published his spiritual masterpiece, *Introduction to the Devout Life*. In this book, he guided readers through detailed meditations designed to help them choose to love and serve God above all else. He encouraged regular prayer and the sacraments and explained very practically how to cultivate virtue and live a moral life. For example, when we find ourselves "surprised into anger," Francis wrote that it is best to "drive it away quickly than to start a discussion with it. If we give it ever so little time, it will become mistress of the place" (Part III, Chapter 8).

Francis' book was so popular that it was soon translated into other languages, and from his poor diocese, the fame of Bishop de Sales spread. Coupled with reports of miraculous healings that occurred through his prayers, Francis was quickly being recognized as a saint.

Francis' second famous book, the *Treatise on the Love of God*, was written in 1616 for people who are "advanced in devotion." The book described a kind of silent, mystical prayer in which "eyes speak to eyes, and heart to heart, and none understand what passes save the sacred lovers who speak" (Book IV, Chapter 1). Such words were not merely theoretical. Francis, Jeanne, and the other Visitation nuns at Annecy were beginning to experience this kind of depth in their own prayer, and the book grew out of their time together when

Francis would present "conferences" to the sisters.

Although he was only middle-aged, it would not be long before Francis would finally see Jesus face to face. The constant stress of his demanding lifestyle contributed to deteriorating health. In 1622, even though he was ill, he accepted an invitation from the Duke of Savoy to attend a church/state conference in Avignon. The Sisters of the Visitation in Lyons could offer only a small, poorly heated room for him to stay, and, despite swelling in his legs, he insisted on walking everywhere he went. On December 26, after spending three hours in the cold at an outdoor service, Francis suffered a cerebral hemorrhage. He died two days later, only fifty-five years old.

By 1656, *Introduction to the Devout Life* had already been translated into seventeen languages. Through the written word—which displays all the gentleness, love and wisdom that made him famous—St. Francis de Sales has pastored millions of Christians. The patron saint of Catholic writers and a Doctor of the Church, he is still attracting others to take the narrow path that leads to Christ.

━◈═ A Magnet for Christ ═◈━

In this selection, taken from Part I,
Chapter 3, of *Introduction to the Devout Life*,
St. Francis de Sales discusses how Christians
in any vocation can practice devotion.
The book is addressed to "Philothea,"
which de Sales said signified a soul in love
with God.

Devotion Is Suitable to Every Kind of
Life-Situation and Occupation

God commanded the plants, at the creation, to bear fruit each according to its kind (Genesis 1:11). Similarly, he commands Christians, the living plants of his Church, to produce the fruits of devotion, according to each one's ability and occupation.

Devotion is to be practiced differently by the nobleman, the workman, the servant, the prince, the widow, the young girl, the wife. Even more than this, the practice of devotion has to be adapted to the strength, life-situation and duties of each individual.

Do you think, dear Philothea, that it is suitable for a bishop to desire to live the life of a hermit like a Carthusian monk? If people with a family were to want to be like the Capuchins not acquiring any property, if a workman spent a great deal of time in church like the member of a religious order, and if a religious was always subject to being disturbed in all sorts of ways for the service of his neighbor like a bishop, would not such devotion be ridiculous, disorderly and intolerable?

However, this sort of fault is very common. The world, which does not distinguish or does not want to distinguish between devotion and the indiscretion of those who consider themselves devout, complains and finds fault with devotion which is in no way responsible for such disorders.

Indeed, Philothea, devotion in no way spoils anything if it be true, rather it makes everything perfect. When it conflicts with any person's legitimate occupation, it is without doubt false. "The bee," says Aristotle, "sucks honey from flowers without damaging them," leaving them as whole and fresh as it found them. But true devotion does even better. Not only does it not spoil any sort of life-situation or occupation, but on the contrary enriches it and makes it attractive. All sorts of precious stones when immersed in honey have a greater brilliance, each according to its color. Similarly, everyone becomes more pleasant in one's state of life by joining it with devotion.

Devotion makes the care of the family peaceful, the love of husband and wife more sincere, the service of the ruler more loyal, and every sort of occupation more pleasant and more loveable.

It is an error, or rather, a heresy, to try to exclude the devout life from the soldiers' regiment, the workmen's shop, the court of rulers or the home of the married. It is true, Philothea, that a devotion which is purely contemplative, monastic and religious cannot be practiced in such occupations. However, besides these three sorts of devotion, there are many others suitable for leading to perfection those who live their lives in the world. This is attested in the Old Testament by Abraham, Isaac and Jacob, David, Job, Tobias, Sara, Rebecca and Judith.

In the New Testament, St. Joseph, Lydia (Acts 16:14-15) and St. Crispin lived perfectly devout lives in their workshop, St. Anne, St. Martha, St. Monica, Aquila and Priscilla (Acts 18:1-4) in their family; Cornelius (Acts 10), St. Sebastian, St. Maurice in the army; Constantine, Helen, St. Louis, [King of France, 1227-1270], Blessed Amadeus [Duke of Savoy, 1465-1472], and St. Edward [the Confessor, King of England, 1042-1066] on the throne. It has even happened that many have lost perfection while in solitude, even though it is so favorable for perfection. Others have retained it amidst the multitude which seems of such little help for perfection. As St. Gregory mentions, Lot who was chaste while living in the city was defiled while in the desert. No matter where we are, we can and we should seek a life of perfection.

The Life of Francis de Sales

1567 - Born at Thorens in Savoy on August 21

1581-88 - Studies at the Jesuit College in Paris

1586 - Experiences brief spiritual crisis

1588-92 - Studies law and theology at the University of Padua

1593 - Ordained on December 18 and appointed provost of diocese

1594-98 - Missionary work in Chablais

1599 - Appointed coadjutor to the Bishop of Geneva

1602 - Visits Paris on diplomatic mission; consecrated Bishop of Geneva on December 8

1604 - Preaches Lenten sermons at Dijon and meets Jeanne de Chantal

1607 - Begins plans to found new religious order

1609 - *Introduction to the Devout Life* published

1610 - Institute of the Visitation is founded with Jeanne de Chantal as its superior

1616 - *Treatise on the Love of God* published

1622 - Dies at Lyons on December 28

1665 - Canonized by Pope Alexander VII on April 19

1877 - Declared a Doctor of the Church on July 7

Go to the Poor

Dorothy Day
1897 - 1980

*Hardly a seminarian of my era escaped her influence.
Rare was the young priest untouched by her life. Whether
or not we honored in our own lives her passionate
commitment to the poor, or followed even distantly in her
footsteps, she worried us. That was her gift to us, a gift I
still cherish.*
  —Cardinal John O'Connor of New York

When Cardinal O'Connor
proposed the idea of sainthood for Dorothy Day in November
1997—one hundred years after her birth—he portrayed a
woman who spoke out courageously against injustice, even
when it made people uncomfortable.

Cofounder of the Catholic Worker movement, Dorothy
Day combined the practice of Christian charity with the struggle for social justice. Through her criticism of the economic
and social structures that trap people in poverty, Day awakened Catholics—and Christians everywhere—to the need to
change the conditions that exploit the vulnerable. A deep
inner faith life, which she nourished with prayer, Scripture

and the sacraments, sustained her as she lived out the call that God had give to her to care for the poor and destitute.

The Stirrings of a Vocation

Long before she converted to Catholicism, Dorothy Day was concerned with the gross inequities she saw around her. Born on November 8, 1897 in Brooklyn, New York, she lived most of her childhood in relative comfort. As a teenager, she was so affected by Upton Sinclair's *The Jungle* that she took long walks from her middle class Chicago neighborhood to the poor tenement districts Sinclair had described. Her family was not religious, but she often found herself thinking about God. She began attending an Episcopal Church periodically with a neighbor and nurtured a love for the Psalms.

In 1914, at the age of sixteen, Day won a scholarship to the University of Illinois at Urbana, where she met friends who shared her concerns about the problems of society. When her family moved back to New York two years later, she left the university and found a reporting job for a socialist newspaper in the city.

A New York Radical

Over the next few years, Day worked on several labor newspapers and spent her free time with a radical, literary group of friends in Greenwich Village. At the age of twenty, she was jailed for several weeks for picketing on behalf of the women's suffrage movement. She fell desperately in love with an ex-newspaperman and became pregnant with a child he didn't want. In a desperate attempt to keep the two of them together, Day had an abortion. But it didn't work. He deserted her, leaving her desolate. Several months later, on the rebound, she married an older man, but the union lasted only a year. After taking reporting jobs in Chicago and New Orleans, she returned to New York in 1924 and met the man who would become her common-law husband, Forster Batterham.

Ironically, it was the happiness Day felt with Batterham and the joy of expecting their child that led her to the Lord. During her pregnancy, she found herself praying, "and, encouraged that I was praying because I wanted to thank Him, I went on praying." She began to attend a Catholic Mass regularly, but her attraction to religion became a source of tension between herself and Forster, who was an atheist.

When their daughter Tamar was born in March of 1927, Dorothy Day had the baby baptized, and this caused even more tension. She knew she could not remain with Forster if she became a Catholic; he would not agree to any marriage ceremony either before the state or the church. She loved him intensely, and she later wrote, "It was killing me to think of leaving him." The couple finally separated, however, and Dorothy was baptized into the Catholic Church.

Siding with the "Opposition"

Dorothy's acceptance of the Lord and her entrance into the church also meant losing her radical friends. They thought that she had "gone over to the opposition, because of course the Church was lined up with property, with the wealthy, with the state, with capitalism." In many ways, she agreed. "There was plenty of charity but too little justice," she once wrote about the church.

And yet, Day possessed a deep inner conviction that Jesus lived in his church. "The priests were the dispensers of the Sacraments, bringing Christ to men, all enabling us to put on Christ and to achieve more nearly in the world a sense of peace and unity."

For several years, Day continued writing while caring for Tamar. After covering a demonstration in Washington, D.C. in 1932, she went to the National Shrine of the Immaculate Conception and offered up a prayer, "a prayer which came with tears and with anguish, that some way would open up for me to use what talents I possessed for my fellow workers, the poor." When she arrived home, she found a poorly dressed French immigrant waiting for her.

It was Peter Maurin, a Catholic man with revolutionary ideas for a new social order that would begin with each person living out Jesus' command to love one another. It would be up to every individual—not the government—to care for those in need. Maurin's vision included a life of voluntary poverty—everyone taking less so that others could have more. He emphasized the dignity of the worker and of work, and believed this dignity could be more fully realized when people worked the land rather than slaving in huge factories.

The Catholic Worker

Part of Maurin's plan called for publishing a newspaper to discuss these ideas and to educate Catholics on the church's social teachings. He had read Day's articles, and knew she could help him. With fifty-seven dollars Dorothy scraped up, the two published the first issue of *The Catholic Worker* in May 1933. The twenty-five hundred copies were sold on the streets for a penny a piece. Their paper struck a chord with Catholics suffering through the worst depression in American history, and by 1936, the circulation had soared to 150,000.

At the same time, Maurin and Day set up a "house of hospitality"—based on the Christian "hospices" of the Middle Ages—to feed the destitute and shelter them as long as they wished to stay. As the Worker paper spread the news of the movement, volunteers came to staff the houses, and other communities were established across the country. By 1941, thirty-one houses were operating, in addition to several farming communes.

It was exciting work, but it was also difficult. Voluntary poverty meant living in run-down houses and among people from the streets who could be rude, drunk, mentally ill, or even dangerous. There was little privacy or quiet. While Day's sharp intellect and idealism had led her to see a solution for the problems of society in Maurin's gospel-based vision, it would be her faith that would enable her over the years to carry out this commitment.

Prayer, Pacifism, and Jail

Day lived an intensely religious life. She loved Scripture, and at her lowest moments, she would retreat to her room in near desperation to immerse herself in the Bible. "The Bible helps me get through the painful times of this life, reminds me of what I am doing here," she once said. Her favorite passage was chapter twelve of the Book of Romans, which she saw as sanctioning the idea of community life. The saints were her friends from whom she drew strength for the struggles she knew they had also faced. She went to Mass nearly every day.

Dorothy Day was unswervingly faithful to the church's doctrinal teachings, but in politics she did not shrink from controversy. At one time, she sided with gravediggers in a strike against the diocese of New York. Her pacifist stance lost many supporters for the Worker cause, especially during World War II, but she was convinced that her position on nonviolence was based on Jesus' command to love even our enemies. She was jailed in the 1950s for not taking part in air raid drills.

As the Worker movement became better known, Dorothy traveled around the country giving speeches, supporting worker strikes, and writing firsthand about the poverty and hopelessness that littered the land. Although she was a controversial figure, her celebrity status often caused her to worry that she would fall victim to the sin of pride.

Pressing on in Faith

Dorothy Day lived the better part of her last fifty years in Worker communities on the Lower East Side of New York, where she continued the work she had begun with Peter Maurin. Even at the age of seventy-five, she was arrested for a farm worker protest. She died on November 29, 1980, when she was eighty-three years old.

"What we would like to do is change the world—make it a little simpler for people to feed, clothe, and shelter themselves as God intended them to do," Dorothy wrote in a 1946 *Catholic Worker* column. "But," she added, "the more we do, the more we realize that the most important thing is to love." Dorothy Day loved her neighbor in a radical way. "She was a radical," said Cardinal O'Connor, "precisely because she was a believer, a believer and a practitioner." And as with all believers who have walked so closely with Christ, her words and example continue to challenge us today.

Go to the Poor

Dorothy Day wrote this editorial for a May
1942 issue of *The Catholic Worker,*
which marked the beginning of the tenth year
of the newspaper's existence.

This is an editorial for "little ones," for the poor, the
meek, the suffering. I am writing it as I sit in St.
Bibiana's Cathedral in Los Angeles, a place of joy and
beauty, set in the slums of a great city.

How wonderful that it should be here, surrounded by the
poor—yes not only by the poor, but the degraded and the lost
ones of this world. Christ chose a stable as a place to be born
in. So how He must love to be here.

Outside, on Second and Main streets in Los Angeles,
there are pawnshops, saloons, burlesque shows, flophouses.
It is the "Skid road" of the city, like our Bowery in New York.
Inside, there is beauty and quiet and many bowed in prayer
at early Mass.

Pope Leo XIII said the workers were lost to the Church.
Pope Pius XI said to his priests: "Go to the poor."

Our Lord walked the highways and byways, dusty and
tired, to teach His brothers whom "God so loved." The closer
we are to the poor, the closer to Christ's love.

Go to Mary

Mary was poor. St. Bonaventure, in his life of Christ, said
St. Joseph was so poor that he could not earn enough even
for the simple wants of the Holy Family, so the Blessed Mother

took in sewing. Oh Mother of beautiful love, of fear, of knowledge and of holy hope, teach us to be poor, ever to have less so that others may have more, always to be the little, the fools of this earth. Our Lord God, Creator of the world, was born in a stable. Lend us your heart, and come to the stable of our bodies, bearing our Lord to us, loving Him, praising Him, adoring Him for us.

A New Year

This editorial, marking the beginning of the tenth year of *The Catholic Worker*, is for all I met this month, all those families on the march, those soldiers going to and from leave, those prisoners I met at the reformatory at El Keno, for all our readers everywhere, the little and the poor.

It is to all of us that the Church comes, "calling attention to our high vocation as Christians, and to the great tasks, the conflicts and sufferings which confront us in the Kingdom of God" (Short Breviary, page 5, footnote).

We are the sons of God, believing in His Name, and we bring messages of prayer and penance (Father Hugo), and messages of peace (Father Orchard), messages to a world at war, a world to which penance is foolishness, and peace, treason.

We enter a new year with this month of May, and we enter with a joyful spirit, mindful of the love of God for us, and the love we should bear for all, friend and foe, English, Russian, Chinese, Japanese, and Germans. They are our brothers, and love for them is "the fulfilling of the law." Love is "the measure by which we shall be judged," and that love is to be shown by works of mercy, not by war.

St. Paul's Message

"Put ye on therefore, brethren, the bowels of mercy, benignity, humility, modesty, patience: bearing with one another and forgiving one another, if any have a complaint against another: even as the Lord hath forgiven you, so do you also. But above all these things, have charity, which is the bond of perfection: and let the peace of Christ rejoice in your hearts, wherein also you are called in one body (Colossians 3:12-15).

The Life of Dorothy Day

1897 - Born on November 8 in Brooklyn, New York

1904 - Dorothy's family moves to San Francisco area

1906 - Following San Francisco earthquake, the family moves to Chicago

1914 - Enters the University of Illinois at Urbana

1916 - Leaves the University and finds job as reporter for a socialist New York City paper

1917 - Jailed for picketing in Washington, D.C. on behalf of women's suffrage movement

1918 - Falls in love with ex-newspaperman

1919 - Has an abortion; her lover deserts her

1920 - Marries older man; divorces him after one year

1924 - Meets Forster Batterham, who becomes her common-law husband

1927 - Dorothy's daughter Tamar born on March 3; breaks up with Batterham and enters the Catholic Church on December 28

1932 - Reports on a protest march in Washington, D. C., and prays that God would use her to help the poor; the next day meets Peter Maurin

1933 - First edition of *The Catholic Worker* published on May 1; first house of hospitality opened

1936 - Catholic Worker houses established across country

1941-1945 - *The Catholic Worker* maintains pacifist stance during Word War II, losing many supporters

1955 - Dorothy sent to jail for refusing to take part in civil defense drills

1973 - Jailed for protesting farmworkers' plight, marking last time she is sent to prison

1980 - Dies on November 29

Guardian of His Flock

Saint Thomas Becket

1118 - 1170

After six years in exile in France, Thomas Becket, Archbishop of Canterbury, was back in England and headed once more for his cathedral. His flock rejoiced at his homecoming, lining the road before him with their cloaks and crying, "Blessed is he who comes in the name of the Lord."

A month later, the fragile peace he had reached with his rival, King Henry II, was already unraveling. It seemed inevitable that the competing authorities of church and throne would continue to clash. Becket's excommunication of several bishops who sided with the king, along with nobles who held church lands unlawfully, made Henry and his barons furious.

Four barons decided to take action, once and for all, to rid England of this man. On Tuesday, December 29, 1170, they confronted Becket in the Archbishop's palace and ordered him to absolve the bishops or leave the kingdom. "Never," Thomas replied. "Once I behaved like a timid priest and left England. I have not come back in order to flee.

If I am allowed to perform the duties of the priesthood in peace, I shall be glad; if not, God's will be done with me."

Thomas' monks hurried him into the cathedral, where they thought he would be safe from violence. The knights burst through the heavy doors of the great church. They tried to take Thomas prisoner, but he resisted. When one knight whirled his sword over his head, Thomas stopped fighting. After two blows to the head, he prayed. After several more blows, Thomas Becket was dead.

A Defender of the Church

What sort of dispute between a high churchman and his king could end in murder? For Thomas, the issue was the very life of the church in England. How could an archbishop properly care for his people if the king held the right to select bishops, seize church lands and revenue, and require state consent to excommunicate land holders or even to visit the Pope? Thomas believed he could not pastor his clergy when they could be tried and punished in civil rather than church courts. To compromise these principles meant compromising his calling. Thomas loved God too much to abandon his church and his people.

Ironically, Thomas was a close friend and trusted adviser of Henry's before they became enemies. He was born in London in 1118, the son of a merchant, and educated in a monastery. His summers were spent on a baron's estate, learning the ways of the nobility. After studying law in Paris, he returned to London and eventually became a deacon in the Archbishop of Canterbury's household. His exceptional church service won him recognition, and when the twenty-one-year-old Henry ascended the throne in 1154, he appointed thirty-six-year-old Thomas as chancellor.

Thomas threw himself wholeheartedly into his King's service. His lavish lifestyle brought him both praise and criticism. While living austerely himself, he held back nothing from his guests. It was said that the chancellor's household served the best wines but that the chancellor himself drank only boiled water. As a young man, he had taken a vow of chastity, yet his strikingly tall figure often sported the most fashionable clothing. He entertained with such grace and style that an invitation to Thomas' household was more sought after than the king's. He personally led the royal army in Toulouse, France, to victory over disputed land. Clearly, this was not the usual behavior of a deacon!

In England, church and state had been deeply entwined for many years. Under the feudal system of government, monarchs gave land to people, both lay and cleric, in return for certain services, such as revenue and defense. In the eleventh century, however, spiritual reform resulted in a strong papacy with centralized authority over the clergy.

When Henry offered Thomas the archbishop's post in 1162, he was reluctant to accept it, warning the king that he would have to serve God above royalty. For Henry, however, there was no difference between service to the church and service to the state. He wanted Thomas to be archbishop and chancellor at the same time. An archbishop who was also chancellor would help Henry regain the state's eroding control over the church. But when Thomas accepted the archbishopric, he resigned as chancellor, a move which both surprised and insulted the king.

Full Surrender to Christ

In this transition from statesman to churchman, Thomas experienced a deep conversion. Although his behavior had never been scandalous, his ostentatious lifestyle and obvious ambition were evidence of a shallow commitment to the Lord. When he became archbishop, however, Thomas knew he served no higher master and he strove to become worthy of the honor. He rose before dawn each morning, said the Divine Office, and privately washed the feet of thirteen poor men. He said Mass with great reverence, and wore simple monastic clothing over a hair shirt. Thomas' loyalties were no longer divided—he had fully surrendered himself to Christ.

Disputes with the king began almost immediately. If Henry had believed that Thomas, his good friend, would continue to do as he asked, he quickly realized he was mistaken. Thomas ardently defended the church and her rights. Henry felt betrayed by a man he had raised up from a "low" birth to become the second most powerful person in England. To Henry, Thomas was profoundly ungrateful.

Henry asked Thomas to swear that he would abide by the ancient customs that had prevailed between church and state. Thomas and his bishops agreed but included in their oath of loyalty the phrase, "saving my order," meaning they would observe the customs as long as they did not conflict with their obligations to the church. At a meeting in Clarendon in 1164, Henry asked the bishops to sign sixteen declarations, known as "constitutions," which put in writing the controls over the church which the king desired. When spelled out, these went much farther than Thomas had imagined. He accepted a copy of them, which signaled his assent, but immediately regretted his action. Leaving the council deeply saddened, Thomas refused to put his final seal on the document. He wrote to the Pope, asking to be forgiven for turning his back on the church.

The Sword and the Cross

Henry was so angered at Thomas for challenging his authority that he summoned the archbishop to a trial on trumped-up charges of embezzlement. Sensing that martyrdom might be the outcome of the dispute, Thomas celebrated a special Mass to honor St. Stephen the Martyr. He arrived at the trial at Northampton castle, holding a heavy cross before him. His opponent, the bishop of London, Gilbert Foliot, feared a confrontation between sword and cross and warned Thomas: "If the king draws his sword and you brandish your cross, there will be a disaster." Thomas replied, "My cross is a sign of peace for myself and the English Church."

The trial was the breaking point of the crisis. Before the sentence of treason could be declared, Thomas rose from his seat and hurriedly left the castle. Shouts of "traitor" filled the hall, along with threats of violence.

Feeling that his life was in danger, Thomas escaped in disguise and sought refuge in France. He spent the next six years in monasteries, immersing himself in prayer. During this difficult time, he prepared his soul for what he knew might be the ultimate sacrifice—martyrdom. Thomas continually sought help from the Pope and the bishops in England, but all attempts at negotiation failed.

Finally, a fragile agreement was reached, and Thomas returned to England. On Christmas Day, as he preached to the crowds in the cathedral, Thomas predicted that they would soon lose their spiritual father. Henry had become alarmed over reports that Thomas was traveling with armed knights—although they were for his protection, not for a planned uprising. The king was also fuming over Thomas' excommunications of two bishops who were supporting the throne. Barons who were siding with the king assumed that Henry wanted Thomas' life. Without the king's permission, four barons took off to arrest the archbishop. What started out as an arrest, however, became a murder in the cathedral itself.

Victory for the Church

When the king learned of Thomas' death, he burst into tears and shut himself up in his room for three days. In friendship and in enmity, Henry had never stopped caring for Thomas. He swore on the Bible that he did not order the death, but took responsibility for his part in inciting the barons. In repentance, he renounced the Clarendon constitutions. Thomas had shed his blood, and the church had its victory.

Two days after Thomas Becket died, the wife of a knight who had made a vow to "Thomas the Martyr" was healed of blindness. Numerous miracles followed, and only three years later, the archbishop was canonized. For hundreds of years thereafter, Canterbury was a mecca for pilgrims, who knelt at the site of Thomas' martyrdom and prayed for his intercession. Even the barons who killed him later repented and built a hospital and a monastery in his honor. Thomas became the shepherd who cared so much for his sheep that, like Christ, he was willing to lay down his life for them. Even his enemies came to admire this man who had stood for his church and, like a knight, defended it to his death.

Guardian of His Flock

Edward Grim, a monk, observed the attack on the Archbishop in the cathedral, came to his aid, and was wounded himself. He wrote this eye-witness account some years later. This selection begins after the knights have stormed into the cathedral.

The murderers followed him [Archbishop Thomas Becket]; "Absolve," they cried, "and restore to communion those whom you have excommunicated, and restore their powers to those whom you have suspended."

He answered, "There has been no satisfaction, and I will not absolve them."

"Then you shall die," they cried, "and receive what you deserve."

"I am ready," he replied, "to die for my Lord, that in my blood the Church may obtain liberty and peace. But in the name of Almighty God, I forbid you to hurt my people whether cleric or lay."

Then they lay sacrilegious hands on him, pulling and dragging him that they may kill him outside the church, or carry him away a prisoner, as they afterwards confessed. But when he could not be forced away from the pillar, one of them pressed on him and clung to him more closely. Him he pushed off, calling him "pander" and saying, "Touch me not, Reginald; you owe me fealty and subjection; you and your accomplices act like madmen."

The knight, fired with a terrible rage at this severe

repulse, waved his sword over the sacred head. "No faith," the knight cried, "nor subjection do I owe you against my fealty to my lord the king."

Then the unconquered martyr seeing the hour at hand which should put an end to this miserable life and give him straightway the crown of immortality promised by the Lord, inclined his neck as one who prays and joining his hands he lifted them up, and commended his cause and that of the Church to God, to St. Mary, and to the blessed martyr Denis. Scarce had he said the words than the wicked knight, fearing lest he should be rescued by the people and escape alive, leapt upon him suddenly and wounded this lamb who was sacrificed to God on the head, cutting off the top of the crown which the sacred unction of the chrism had dedicated to God; and by the same blow he wounded the arm of him who tells this. For he, when the others, both monks and clerks, fled, stuck close to the sainted archbishop and held him in his arms till the one he interposed was almost severed.

Then he received a second blow on the head but still stood firm. At the third blow he fell on his knees and elbows, offering himself a living victim, and saying in a low voice, "For the Name of Jesus and the protection of the Church I am ready to embrace death."

Then the third knight inflicted a terrible wound as he lay, by which the sword was broken against the pavement, and the crown which was large was separated from the head. The fourth knight prevented any from interfering so that the others might freely perpetrate the murder.

As to the fifth, no knight but that clerk who had entered with the knights, that a fifth blow might not be wanting to the martyr who was in other things like to Christ, he put his foot on the neck of the holy priest and precious martyr, and, horrible to say, scattered his brain and blood over the pavement, calling out to the others, "Let us away, knights; he will rise no more."

The Life of Thomas Becket

1118 - Born in London, the son of a merchant

1136 - Goes to Paris to study

1140 - Returns to London and works for sheriff

1141 - Joins household of Archbishop Theobald of
Canterbury

1145 - Spends time in Italy and France studying law

1154 - Appointed archdeacon by Archbishop Theobald; in
December, appointed chancellor by King Henry II

1161 - Archbishop Theobald dies

1162 - Ordained priest June 2; made Archbishop of
Canterbury on June 3 by King Henry; resigns as
chancellor

1164 - *January 3*: Accepts but then refuses to put final seal
on Constitutions of Clarendon, angering the king
October 13: Trumped-up embezzlement trial at
Northampton Council; Thomas escapes to France
and remains in exile for six years

1170 - *December 1*: Fragile reconciliation reached with King
Henry and Thomas returns to England
December 25: Thomas predicts his martyrdom
December 29: Murdered in Canterbury Cathedral by
four barons

1173 - Canonized on February 21.

That All May Be One

Paul Couturier

1881 - 1953

Paul Couturier did not discover his full vocation until he had lived for more than half a century. At a time in his life when most people would be settling into their calling and even begin looking toward retirement, this humble, aging priest with no influence or connections to speak of became one of the twentieth century's greatest apostles of Christian unity. Yves Congar, another renowned ecumenist, once said that Couturier gave the ecumenical movement "its heart of love and prayer." Congar went on, "It was [Couturier] who, spiritually, founded that immense movement which, today, bears the ecumenical hope of the world."

Paul Couturier was born in Lyons, France, on July 29, 1881, into a family of middle-class industrialists. He received the upbringing and education typical of the people of his day until, at the age of nineteen, he decided to dedicate his life to Christ in the priesthood. He entered the Society of St. Irenaeus and was ordained in 1906. Even early on in his priesthood, "Abbé Paul" had a deep reverence for the Mass and a profound sense of the power of prayer—qualities that matured and burned within him for the rest of his life.

After ordination, Abbé Paul was assigned to teach science at the *Institut des Chartreux*, the college that his society ran. Couturier held this position for forty years, even as he became increasingly involved in the work of ecumenism. Further, though the priests of St. Irenaeus normally lived together in community, Abbé Paul's situation called for something different. His only sister, Marie Antoinette, was in poor health and could not live alone, and so he was allowed to live with her in a simple flat in the city. Every evening, when all his brothers in the Lord gathered for the evening meal and fellowship, Paul went off to his sister's apartment and looked after her.

A New Vocation Awakens

When he was in his early forties, it was suggested to Couturier by a retreat master that he expand beyond his work as a teacher and begin help caring for refugees who had fled the Bolshevik Revolution. Through this work, Couturier came to know many Orthodox Christians who had established a Russian colony in Lyons.

For twelve years, Couturier gave these destitute Russians whatever time he could spare from his duties as a teacher. This ministry of charity awakened in him a desire to see all Christians come together in love and mutual service. The words of one Orthodox archbishop from Kiev found a home in his heart: "The walls of separation do not reach the sky."

In 1932, Couturier's visit to a Benedictine priory in Belgium that was dedicated to Christian unity only confirmed

what was growing in his heart. It was there that he discovered the writings of Cardinal Désiré Joseph Mercier, an
early ecumenist who wrote: "In order to unite, we must love
one another; to love one another, we must know one
another; to know one another, we must go and meet one
another." This was already happening in Couturier's life, and
he longed to see it happen to all Christians.

At the priory, Couturier also became aware of the limitations of the Octave of Prayer for Christian Unity, which had
been established with the aim of asking God to guide
Anglicans back to Roman Catholicism. Couturier adapted the
octave to encompass the unity of all Christians and refocused
it on Jesus' prayer at the Last Supper. He made John 17:21—
"Father, that they may all be one"—its spiritual anchor. In
1933, Couturier launched this revised observance in Lyons,
and from that point on, he devoted his life to promoting the
week of prayer throughout the world. He wrote articles, distributed tracts, and invited guest speakers—all with the
goal of encouraging Christians to pray together for the unity
that he knew Jesus so desired.

United with Christ in Prayer

In an era when it was still uncommon for Christians of
different denominations to associate with one another,
Couturier felt that not only should they pray *for* one another,
they must pray *with* one another. And they should pray "that
the unity of all Christians may come, such as Christ wills and
by the means he wills." Couturier understood that each person has his or her own vision for bringing the church back
together, but he knew that it is only as we all prayerfully lis-

ten to God that we will understand *his* way toward unity. Praying this way would also allow Christians to come together without trying to win one another over to their own denominations.

Faithful to his own Catholic tradition, Couturier called the church his "well-beloved Mother." Yet he had a sensitive understanding and sympathy for other Christian traditions and was quick to see the truths contained in them. He realized that it was not just doctrinal differences that kept Christians separated. Catholics, Orthodox, and Protestants all had painful memories of suffering and humiliation at one another's hands, and attitudes of hostility and suspicion had hardened over centuries.

Couturier felt that these mindsets separating Christians could only be overcome by repentance. He was convinced of the need for Christians to do penance for their pride and lack of charity and to ask forgiveness for the sins that their churches committed against other Christian brothers and sisters. In his own prayer, Couturier was moved by the image of Jesus hanging on the cross in agony, his body torn and broken, suffering the pains of his body on earth—the church torn by division and enmity.

A Circle of Love

Through his efforts to foster what he called "spiritual ecumenism," Couturier developed a wide circle of friendships. He had the warmth and ability to stretch out his hand across denominational boundaries and bring others to share in the cause so close to his heart. He visited England twice and established strong friendships among Anglican clergy and the

Anglican monks from the Community of the Resurrection. In 1940, he was also visited by Roger Schutz, the founder of the ecumenical community of Taizé in France, and he returned the visit in 1941.

While Couturier encouraged serious discussion of ecumenical issues, he always insisted that any dialogue be surrounded by an atmosphere of mutual prayer to avoid tension or sterile debate. His contact with a group of Reformed pastors led to the establishment of the *Groupe des Dombes* which, beginning in 1937, brought together French and Swiss priests and pastors in an annual retreat for prayer and ecumenical discussion.

All the friendships Couturier established grew deeper through a voluminous correspondence. With some friends, he created an "invisible monastery," a spiritual communion of people who, without knowing one another, nevertheless committed themselves to praying together for Christian unity.

All these activities and relationships did not prevent Couturier from giving as much time and money as possible to promoting the Week of Prayer for Christian Unity. As a result of his efforts, the observance was gradually embraced throughout France and beyond. Today, the theme and biblical texts for the worldwide annual Week of Prayer are prepared by a joint committee of the Vatican's Pontifical Council for Promoting Christian Unity and the World Council of Churches' Commission on Faith and Order.

A Far-Reaching Apostolate

Long frail and diabetic, Abbé Paul's health was further undermined by a brief imprisonment in Lyons by the Gestapo during World War II on suspicion of conspiracy. Nonetheless, he energetically carried on his work throughout the late 1940s. Even after he developed a grave heart condition in 1951, Couturier continued his correspondence and celebrated Mass daily in the small chapel he had set up in the flat that he shared with his sister. The Mass plunged him into Jesus' sacrifice on the cross, the center of his faith. It was there that Couturier lived his ecumenical ideal most profoundly—in union with Jesus, the Reconciler of Christians.

When Couturier died on March 24, 1953, at the age of seventy-two, photographs, letters, lists of prayer intentions, and mementos of friends were found on his altar. His wide heart had brought all these people and their needs before the Lord daily in Mass. On the walls of his room hung Catholic, Orthodox, Protestant crosses, Russian icons, and a poster advertising that year's week of prayer. Here was a man absorbed with the desire for Christian unity, a man whose entire life was focused on the goal of bringing together the scattered children of God.

By helping so many people see the need for healing in the body of Christ, Paul Couturier did much to prepare the way for the great work of Vatican II and the ecumenical ventures undertaken since then. As he predicted so prophetically more than half a century ago: "A great miracle is beginning to be performed on the threshold of a new epoch. It is the beginning of the transformation of broken Christianity into a Christianity truly one according to the unity willed by Christ."

That All May Be One

Abbé Paul Couturier printed this statement in 1944, unsigned. During the winter preceding his death in 1952-1953, he republished it in a slightly revised form, with his own signature and the imprimatur of his archbishop. In this second form he regarded it as his "ecumenical testament."

Visible Christian unity will be attained when the praying Christ has found enough Christian souls of all communions for him to pray freely in them to his Father for Unity. The silent voice of Christ must sound forth in the voices of all his baptized, in all their supplications made in humility and penitence—for we all bear a terrible burden of guilt in this drama of separation. If this guilt were only guilt of omission, indifference, unconcern or readiness to accept the present state of affairs, it would be terrible enough; but how much spiritual pride has shown itself, and still shows itself on all sides, strengthening the barriers and deepening the ditches? Let each of us examine himself before God.

Because the Catholic affirms the unique nature of the Catholic Church as an integral part of his Faith, he must be the first to set an example of deep humility, not merely in a passing moment of condescension, but as an habitual expression of his sorrow for broken Christianity—a sorrow which persists as a token of true regret and contrition for the faults of his ancestors, remembering the human history of the Church, at once glorious and full of wretchedness; and remembering also his own faults. It is essential to do this, if his attitude to his beliefs is to be logical; also it will throw the glory of the past into great relief. He is likewise under an obligation, which is inexorable, to take the initiative in a mutual search for imaginative sympathy—the cordial welcome, the outstretched hand, the open and sincere heart, love of one's neighbor in the true, and therefore full sense of the word "He who humbles himself shall be exalted." He who loves, provided that his love is persistent and admits of no exception, is he who in the last resort begets understanding. "Where love is not, set love, and you will receive love back," says St. John of the Cross, echoing the great apostle John: 'We have known and believed the love that God hath to us" (1 John 4:16).

Prayer, the fundamental cosmic force of creation, is found in its completeness in Christ as he prayed for Unity. In that prayer he expressed before his Father his own desire, since Christian Unity is part of his Father's divine plan; his prayer is the expression of his will for his baptized. What has once existed in the mind of Christ exists eternally, for through his mind it becomes part of his person, part of the eternal Word. Christ continues to pray for Unity until the end of time, in the love of the Spirit, the Lamb before the Father's throne. But he desires us to share this prayer with him, for all Christians share his life. Indeed, he has so willed it that he cannot bring about Christian Unity without us, just as he cannot save us without our cooperation. Each of us can take to himself the words of St. Paul, "I make up . . . in my prayer in him for Unity what is lacking in his prayer."

God has created us free, in his own image, making us "free sons in his own Son," and receiving us again into himself by his love; and he could not encroach upon this marvelous gift of freedom without to some extent destroying our personality; far from doing this, he has raised us by the Infinity of the Person of his Anointed One.

Honor and responsibility, thanksgiving and guilt, humility and contrition; such are the two aspects of the human spirit. To hold in our hands the responsibility for Christian Unity—though not for the unity of the Church—to hold such great responsibility that if we were to neglect it, God in his justice would find terrible ways to make us fulfill our role—such is our Christian destiny, as glorious as it is terrifying. But let us take courage; God is love, and he is still our Father.

The Life of Paul Couturier

1881 - Born on July 29 in Lyons, to a middle-class industrialist family

1884-93 - Childhood in French Algeria

1900 - Begins his studies for the priesthood in the Society of St. Ireneaus

1906 - Ordained on June 9 at the cathedral in Lyons

1906-09 - Studies at the Catholic College of Lyons for a degree in Physical Science

1910 - Becomes schoolmaster in the *Institut des Chartreux*

1923-35 - Charitable work among Russian Orthodox refugees in Lyons

1932 - Spends month of July at the Benedictine Priory of the Monks of Unity

1933 - First observance of the Octave of Unity in January in Lyons

1935 - Publishes an article on the "Psychology of the Octave," which is well-received by Catholics and Protestants and advances his efforts to have the Week of Prayer for Christian Unity more widely recognized

1937 - First visit to England

1938 - Second visit to England

1939 - Makes first contacts with the World Council of Churches

1944 - Imprisoned by the Gestapo at Fort Montuc in Lyons from April 12 to June 12

1948 - Sends memorandum to Pope Pius XII concerning interconfessional theological conferences

1951 - Grave heart trouble begins

1953 - Dies on March 24; funeral on March 27 at the Church of St. Bruno, at which Cardinal Gerlier, Archbishop of Lyons, gives an address

Acknowledgments

Every effort has been made to locate and secure permission for the inclusion of all copyrighted material in this book. If any such acknowledgments have been inadvertently omitted, the publisher would appreciate receiving full information so that proper credit may be given in future editions.

Page 14   From Saint Augustine's *Confessions*, translated by Henry Chadwick, © Oxford University Press, London, 1991. Used by permission of Oxford University Press.

Page 26   From *The Collected Works of St. Teresa of Avila, Volume One*, translated by Kieran Kavanaugh and Otilio Rodriguez, © 1976 by Washington Province of Discalced Carmelites, ICS Publications, 2131 Lincoln Road, N. E., Washington, D. C. Used by permission.

Page 40   From *Blessed Miguel Pro, Twentieth-Century Mexican Martyr*, by Ann Ball, © 1996 by Tan Books and Publishers, Inc., Rockford, Illinois. Used by permission of the author.

Page 52   From *Story of a Soul*, translated by John Clarke, O.C.D, © 1975, 1976 by Washington Province of Discalced Carmelites, ICS Publications, 2131 Lincoln Road, N. E., Washington, D. C. Used by permission.

Page 68   From *The Conferences of the Rev. Pére Lacordaire*, translated from the French by Henry Langdon, P. O'Shea, New York, 1870.

Page 80   From *Early Christian Fathers, Library of Christian Classics*, edited by Cyril C. Richardson. Used by permission of Westminster John Knox Press, Louisville, Kentucky.

Page 92   From *Joan of Arc, By Herself and Her Witnesses*, by Regine Pernoud, translated from the French by Edward Hyams, © Macdonald & Co., 1964. 1994 edition, Scarborough House. Used by permission of Scarborough House, Lanham, Maryland.

Page 104   From *Mary MacKillop, An Extraordinary Australian*, by Paul Gardiner S.J., © 1993 by Paul Gardiner S. J. Published by E. J. Dwyer Ltd., Newtown, NSW, Australia.

Page 116   From *Ignatius Loyola, Spiritual Exercises and Selected Works,* edited by George E. Ganss, S.J., © 1991 by George E. Ganss, S.J. Used by permission of Paulist Press.

Page 128   From *Birgitta of Sweden, Life and Selected Revelations*, edited by Marguerite Jader Harris, translated by Albert Ryle Kezel, © 1990 by the Order of St. Birgitta, Rome; translation © 1990 by Albert Ryle Kezel. Used by permission of Paulist Press.

Page 140   From *Saint Anthony Mary Claret, Autobiography,* edited by José Maria Vinas, C.M.F., © 1976 by Claretian Publications, Chicago, Illinois. Used by permission.

Page 152   From the encyclical *Slavorum Apostoli, Eleventh Centenary of Saints Cyril and Methodius*, by Pope John Paul II, published on June 2, 1985.

Page 166   From *Introduction to the Devout Life,* by Saint Francis de Sales. Translated and edited by Fr. Armind Nazareth, M.S.F.S., Fr. Antony Mookenthottam, M.S.F.S., Fr. Antony Kolencherry, M.S.F.S., Malleswaram, Bangalore, India © S.F.S. Publications, 1990. Used by permission.

Page 178   From *The Catholic Worker*, May 1942, taken from the website *Dorothy Day Library on the Web* at http:/www.catholicworker.org/dorothyday/.

Page 192   From *The Murder of Thomas Becket,* taken from Eyewitnesses, Ibis Communications, © 1997 by Ibis Communications (www.ibiscom.com). Used by permission of Ibis Communications.

Page 204   From *Paul Couturier and Unity in Christ*, by Geoffrey Curtis, published by J. William Eckenrode, Westminster, Maryland, © 1964.

Other Resources From The Word Among Us Press

A Great Cloud of Witnesses—The Stories of 16 Saints and Christian Heroes by Leo Zanchettin and Patricia Mitchell
   A companion to *I Have Called You by Name*. Includes practical, down-to-earth biographies of sixteen saints and heroes of the faith. Also features selections of the saints' own writings and time lines to provide historical context.

In the Land I Have Shown You—The Stories of 16 Saints and Christian Heroes from North America by Jeanne Kun
   See how the Lord has been working in the United States and Canada through the lives of our own Saints and Christian heros! Includes: Venerable Pierre Toussaint, Henriette Delille, Saint Rose Philippine Duchesne, Saint Marguerite Bourgeoys and many more— 16 in all, complete with historic time lines and excerpts written by these pioneers of the faith.

Titles in the Companions for the Journey Series

Praying with Anthony of Padua	Praying with Frédéric Ozanam
Praying with Benedict	Praying with Hildegard of Bingen
Praying with C.S. Lewis	Praying with Ignatius of Loyola
Praying with Catherine McAuley	Praying with John Cardinal Newman
Praying with Catherine of Siena	Praying with John of the Cross
Praying with Clare of Assisi	Praying with Mother Teresa
Praying with Dominic	Praying with Pope John the XXIII
Praying with Dorothy Day	Praying with Teresa of Ávila
Praying with Elizabeth Seton	Praying with Thérèse of Lisieux
Praying with Francis of Assisi	Praying with Thomas Aquinas
Praying with Francis de Sales	Praying with Vincent de Paul

From the Wisdom Series:

Divine Love Came Down! Wisdom from Saint Alphonsus Liguori

A Radical Love: Wisdom from Dorothy Day

Live Jesus! Wisdom from Saints Francis de Sales and Jane de Chantal

Love Songs: Wisdom from St. Bernard of Clairvaux

Even Unto Death: Wisdom from Modern Martyrs

   These popular books include short biographies of the authors and selections from their writings grouped around themes such as prayer, forgiveness, and mercy.

To order call 1-800-775-9673
www.wordamongus.org